DEPRESSED ANONYMOUS
WORKBOOK

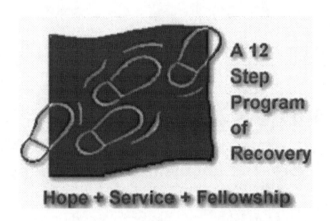

A 12
Step
Program
of
Recovery

Hope + Service + Fellowship

DEPRESSED ANONYMOUS PUBLICATIONS – LOUISVILLE

DEPRESSED ANONYMOUS PUBLICATIONS
Box 17414
Louisville, Kentucky 40217

Web site   http://www.depressedanon.com
Email   depanon@netpenny.net

ISBN 1-929438-00-1

THE DEPRESSED ANONYMOUS WORKBOOK©

INTRODUCTION

All quotes in this **Depressed Anonymous Workbook** which are followed by a capital M in parentheses a r e references to a passage in **The Depressed Anonymous** Manual. The Workbook and the Manual are coordinated so as to help the reader best achieve the goals of their recovery.

While studying the **Workbook** it is a good idea to write out our personal feelings and thoughts in another notebook. These notes can help us see the personal changes that have been accomplished as we move from one step to the next. It is also recommended that the date of each new entry is added in this notebook. Writing out one's responses to the questions in the **Workbook** c a n help you see in black and white how you were thinking and feeling at any particular time.

THE GOAL OF THE WORKBOOK

The Depressed Anonymous Workbook and one's persistent activity in it can produce the results that will help free us from the prison of depression.

STEP ONE
"WE ADMITTED THAT WE WERE POWERLESS OVER DEPRESSION – THAT OUR LIVES HAD BECOME UNMANAGEABLE."

Step One of Depressed Anonymous.

This is step One of **Depressed Anonymous**. It is our purpose in this workbook to reflect on some of the ways that we can admit we are depressed and begin digging out one step at time.

"You have to admit that you're powerless over this depressed behavior and likewise admit that your life is unmanageable. You don't want to go on living this way. In fact, some days you feel that you just want to lie down and die, but deep inside you there is that Spirit, call it God, Higher Power, or whatever, that keeps you searching for a way out..."[1] (M32)

■1.1 Please write down your feelings about the above statement. Do you feel ashamed to talk about the fact that you are or have been depressed? Or hospitalized for depression? This is my attempt to write down some observations about depression and how to best to deal with it.

First of all, I believe that the way most of the people in our groups deal with depression is to admit, first of all that they are depressed. Once this step has been taken the rest of the healing work can continue. Many persons don't know that they are depressed but they do know that aren't feeling themselves. This is in fact a step in the right direction. Dorothy Rowe in her excellent book "DEPRESSION: THE WAY OUT OF YOUR PRISON" speaks about the six absolute truths that we believe when we are depressed. But before we begin looking at those let's first of all draw a map of our life journey and see just where we are right now.

I am using this workbook primarily because I am depressed, hurting and that I want to begin to feel better. I know that the 12 steps of Alcoholics Anonymous originally were written with the intent of providing them with a way out of their slavery and addiction to alcohol. These simple 12 steps have worked their miracle of sobriety in the millions of lives of its members. I also know that by beginning to get an understanding of the steps and how they work that we are opening up a new chapter for our own life and it's healing.

THE DEPRESSED ANONYMOUS WORKBOOK

So, I admit that I am depressed. Now what do I do? The next thing we do is to ask ourselves how much can I dare admit to myself as to how out of control I really am? How much do I dare tell myself that I have really hit bottom and that I have nowhere to go but to ask for help? I have been afflicted with this tendency all my life to run and hide whenever I was challenged by a task, a relationship or old unpleasant memories that frightened me. I would run and hide. I would be willing to barely admit to myself that what I was feeling wasn't really me. I also came to believe that this sea of gloom that I swam in day after day would one day drown me – the exact day and time just happened to be unknown at the time.

But one of the things that keeps giving me hope at the Depressed Anonymous meetings is the fact of how other people view this experience of their lives as those real challenges that open a new vista – a new way to live out our lives and open up hope before us. One man said that the God of his understanding uses his depression and that painful experience for helping others who are likewise depressed and so he uses his experience to overcome the pain of depression. In other words, God will use your depression to help others. And presently through the workbook and the manual **DEPRESSED ANONYMOUS** you can begin to help yourself.

One of the more powerful experiences and benefits of being a member of Depressed Anonymous is that you will learn that you have the choice as to whether you want to stay depressed or choose to learn the ways to get out of your depression. In fact you will also learn that you also have the opportunity to feel differently, if you so choose.

"We" is the first word of Step One. It is a very important word to remember because it immediately sets us up in a group, a fellowship of people who are having the same difficulty. It also makes us feel that we too are not alone, but that there is someone else out there that is experiencing the same difficulties as you and me.

One of the best parts of being a member of Depressed Anonymous is that we don't have to be alone if we don't want to be. That might sound strange to some of us but we have to admit that what keeps us depressed is our need to keep apart from others... to remain disconnected and isolated. We have a need to be by ourselves and to stay apart from human contact. For to be in contact with others means that we will have to take some risks to make some choices. But when I am depressed and alone I don't have to make as many choices or take any action except to keep isolating myself and staying apart.

One of the major reasons for this Workbook is that it can lead us to serenity and establish some positive directions for our lives. If we really are serious about leaving our pit of despair and wanting to do something positive about it then we will have to take the bull by the horns and get serious about our own lives. I am willing right now to decide to give this 12 step program a whirl. I want to feel differently. I have nothing to lose but my depression and my fear of what might replace it when it is gone!

From what I hear from the other members of the group I have nothing to fear but my fear. I know it sounds simple – because it is. Depression clouds, complicates and confuses our reality. So, the final line is this – we know we are not alone. We are together with others who understand and who know the feeling of sadness and depression.

Once we discover that there is a group of men and women who sincerely care about us that we begin to feel differently. But so often people depressed are so pained that they want relief now – and they can't wait another day for relief. But it doesn't work that way. We are really powerless and we have to just be up front about that. I am powerless over my depression. It has me by the throat and I am immobilized. I really feel the despair of my life now more than ever and just know that another day I can't endure.

But what good is it to admit that our depression has made us feel powerless? I already know that you might say? "That is why I have spent thousands of do11ars on hospitals, doctors, counselors and drugs!" But really for a person to admit that they are powerless is what gives us new power – paradoxically. It's like in the letting go of a death grip on our continued sadness that makes the sadness grow and thrive. But somehow – again I don't know how it all works – when I say I'm defeated, deflated and down and have the 12 steps and the fellowship at my side there is like a small ray of light starting to shine in my mind and heart. It's like saying. I've had it this way all my life – now I'll try it your way!!

OK. Here's the game plan. Now, today, you have the choice of no longer being alone. You cannot go through the rest of your life alone or if you do you may stay depressed. Now what we are asking you to do is to get involved with our Depressed Anonymous group and begin to work the steps. Start now. Today we can begin a change in the way we think, feel and act. We no longer have to feel that we are beat and down for the count.

The word ***powerless*** describes the feeling all of us have felt when we were depressed. We just felt that since we were told we had this chemical imbalance that there was nothing that we could do for ourselves but take our medication and talk with our psychiatrist. It is really the being "sick and tired "of being "sick and tired" that gets us to go for help. When I feel powerless I feel ashamed that I am depressed and that I can't do anything about my depression. I want to feel differently and so what I do is to try and feel better about myself.

My shame of not being in control has paradoxically placed me in more of a state of powerlessness, and feeling hopeless and helpless.

Please comment on the next passage from our manual which states:

...That's the way it is with depression – over the years you get comfortable with feeling miserable, which doesn't mean you like it but that you're just too afraid to risk feeling different.[2] (M32)

■ Can you relate to that and if so please write out your comments.

What I intend today is to write down some thoughts about the following:

Now that I have admitted I am having a difficult time living I want to learn some new avenues that will make my life more enjoyable and much more livable.

I know now that at the point that I think my life is at its lowest point – that is when this program of recovery came into my life. I believe with the Psalmist that once stated that we need to commit ourselves to God, trust in him, and that the God of my understanding will act in my behalf.

When I learn to let go of those persons, mental images, past situations and memories, the better I am able to let God control my life. I find this letting go a fearsome project but nevertheless I find that I must do it – if I want to find hope once again.

Some of the major ways people help build the walls of their depression are to consider themselves worthless, won't allow themselves to get angry, they can't forgive themselves or others, and they believe that life is hard and death is worse. Also, they believe that since bad things happened to them in the past bad things are bound to happen to them again in the future.[3] (M28)

■1.3 Please write down in your notebook your own comments about this passage. Is there anything that you might relate to in this passage!

"OUT OF CONTROL"

I have come to the step program because my life is out of control. Whatever I do or think or say seems to make no difference on the way that I feel right now. I feel out of control, and some other force is in charge of my life. I know also that this force, this power other than myself, this sadness has me captive and somehow I have felt unable to do much about it.

THE DEPRESSED ANONYMOUS WORKBOOK

"IN CONTROL"

Let's use the example of Mary – Mary came to a meeting not long ago and announced that her doctor said she had a chemical imbalance. I do believe this is a doctor's nice way of making you believe that you had nothing to do with your sadness – that you're in no way responsible for this, even though that might be true in a sense – but you are now responsible for finding the way out of depression. And if you take an active role in your own recovery – the answers will begin to come! Depressed Anonymous gives you a great choice on the various ways to tell your story and come to some of your own conclusions why you might be depressed. Anyway, she said what her problem was is not her chemical imbalance but anger at her husband – once she got her anger out about her husband she said she has began to have some better days for once.

I think Mary is feeling more in control now that she is in touch with her feelings of anger – the feelings that went unexpressed for so many years. The feelings that had to be pushed aside and down if she was to not allow herself to get out of control.

SURRENDER/ ADMIT/ ACCEPT

I want to admit that my life has been out of control for many years but now that I am in touch with the truth I believe that my life can begin to be lived out differently.

I can begin to use the 12 steps and begin the task of working myself out of the pit of this depression. I believe that with time and with patience plus the group fellowship and support that I will be able to make some positive strides in feeling differently about myself and my world.

■1.4 How many years, months, days can I am remember being depressed? How far back in time can I remember always feeling sad and wanting to withdraw from others? There is no need to feel bad for wanting to isolate and withdraw. Write out your feelings about these experiences.

■1.5 Write down the number of people whom you have admitted to that you have been depressed. #_____

■1.6 Write down their reactions to your admission.
■1.7 When you feel depressed what do you say to yourself? What action or behavior do you do when you feel this way? Does it promote more isolation or more connected? Please write these out.

THE DEPRESSED ANONYMOUS WORKBOOK

■1.8 Is your life unmanageable more now since you have admitted that you are depressed? Can you tell a difference now that you are admitting that depression is and has been a big problem in your life? YES OR NO? Please write out these experiences.

■1.9 What areas of one's life appear to be more out of control now that you are aware of how depression can isolate a person? What area of one's life appears more manageable now that you are aware of how you can change things around -- choose and so begin to feel differently?

■1.10 Do I feel that by my admitting my depression that this is going to help me get rid of depression. Do I still feel as ashamed as before?

■1.11 When have you most felt powerless over anything in your life? How did you handle your feelings of powerlessness then?

■1.12 How many times have you tried to face a challenge or fear only to find that it wasn't the big problem that you first thought it to be?

■1.13 How often do you feel that because of your depression your life is unmanageable.

THE DEPRESSED ANONYMOUS WORKBOOK

STEP TWO
"CAME TO BELIEVE THAT A POWER GREATER THAN MYSELF COULD RESTORE ME TO SANITY."

Step Two of Depressed Anonymous

In this second step of the workshop we are reminded again that in order to begin the process of recovering from our sadness we have to begin to look into our lives and discover where we need to find our sense of self and our power.

Our depression used to be our power in that it kept us shackled in depression – a veritable prison of despair and isolation. Now we see that the light is about to shine on us and we can begin to develop our belief in a power greater than ourselves who will liberate us for hope.

To believe that I might gain deliverance from my depression is something that I am beginning to live with for the first time in years. I want to believe that with time, work and discussion I will free myself from this depression. I need now to write down a list of the things I want to believe in for the present and future so that I might hope that my life can be different.

BELIEFS THAT I WANT TO CHANGE:
THE SIX IMMUTABLE BELIEFS ACCORDING TO
DR. DOROTHY ROWE.

1. I believed that I was worthless, no-good and that no one would ever like me.
2. That life is terrible and that death is worse.
3. I cannot get angry.
4. Bad things happened to me in the past and so bad things will happen to me in the future.
5. I can never forgive anyone, especially myself.
6. I must envy others while hating myself.[1]
7. _____Add your own!

■2.1 NEW BELIEFS THAT I WANT TO LIVE MY LIFE WITH

A. I believe that I can _____

B. I believe that I can _____

C. I believe that I can _____

THE DEPRESSED ANONYMOUS WORKBOOK

D. I believe that I can _____

"I came to believe..."

In the 12 step program of Depressed Anonymous I am learning to march to a different drummer and whistle a different tune. In fact, the road that I am now traveling down is a road that will gradually lead me out of the dead ends of depression, guilt, listlessness and the old familiar atrophy of my spirit to a new vision of who I am to be and become.

WRITE: what is it that you want to begin to believe about yourself that is different from yourself when depressed? Please list four ways that you are going to gradually change the negative and hopeless way you believe about yourself.

■2.2

■2.3

■2.4

■2.5

Now name and list the people, places, situations, things that have exerted the greatest power over you and your life in the past. The places, persons, and situations can have a positive or negative power over you and your life.

■2.6 PERSONS

■2.7 PLACES

■2.8 SITUATIONS

■2.9 TIDNGS

Now stop and reflect upon the persons, places, situations that you either gave power over you or who had power over you. These four categories are powerful influences in the past which even today may still exert their influence over you. Try and write down how this is perceived by you today. In other words, are these people, situations, places or things still causing your life to feel out of control and unmanageable today? If so why? And if not, why not?

■2.10 WRITE OUT YOUR REACTIONS

Read the following from the manual **Depressed Anonymous**. It states:
"We have given ourselves over to the belief that this growing feeling of helplessness is what must govern our lives, moods and behavior. We have given it license to run roughshod over every part of our life and over our relationships. Most people can't see inside us and discover the pain that

makes up our every waking moment. For the most part we are able to hide how miserable we feel.[2] **(M39)**

■2.11 Please write out your comments about the above statement.
LIST THE AREAS OF MY LIFE WHERE I FEEL HELPLESS

■2.12 Write out what I can and must do to change these beliefs.
... A POWER GREATER THAN OURSELVES.

So far my life has been ruled by my sadness, my wanting to withdraw and isolate myself. It seems that my power starts and ends in my head but it is not a power that can relieve me from the hurt of my anguished sadness

As a child I had a particular way at looking at God as our Higher Power. I now want to write down *seven* characteristics of the God of my youth. Describe this God with seven descriptive words.

■2.13.1

■2.13.2

■2.13.3

■2.13.4

■2.13.5

■2.13.6

■2.13.7

■2.14 What do these descriptive words tell me about how I see God?

ARTMIX

Use whatever medium of art (clay, crayons, paints, magic markers, picture collage) that you most feel comfortable with too best describe your relationship with your Higher Power. Also write or describe by whatever means your relationship with whatever your Higher Power may be. For some, it may be God, for some the bottle, sex, food, depressed thoughts, or whatever.

■2.15 DESCRIBE HOW YOUR HIGHER POWER MIGHT BE YOUR DEPRESSION OR YOUR ATTACHMENT TO A PERSON, SUBSTANCE, PLACE, THING OR BEHAVIOR.

For the depressed person, giving up old ways of thinking and acting is much like giving up any other addiction – at first letting go of the old behavior makes you feel uncomfortable. The old behavior wants to cling to our spirit like swamp mud hangs on to knee-high boots. Before your participation in DA you would go home from work, get by yourself and ruminate on how bad you felt. This new behavior will help you think differently about yourself. You will find that this higher power, or God as you understand Him, is not the same God that you might have met when you were young. When you were a child you came to believe that god was watching you, ready to punish you if you were not perfect. You will begin to develop an adult and new way of being related to God as you understand him. With time, persistence and patience you will gradually trust your life to this Higher Power.[3] *(M48)*

Please write out you comments on the above statement.

And the step continues and states:

"...CAN RESTORE ME TO SANITY."

Now that I am beginning to make an effort that this higher Power is really on my side the more my faith and belief will help me overcome my fear of failure that of my depression ever coming to an end.

My fears, anxieties and other obstacles to my serenity will gradually disappear the more I learn that there is somebody up there that loves me and wants me to be free from the gnawing emptiness that continually plagues me day after day. I am beginning to see that the more I attend meetings and read my DA big book, and do my daily meditations the more peace and hope I will have that life will indeed get better for me. My sanity and my health will increase like a seed watered, nurtured and which received a lot of sunlight.

We aren't alone anymore. In fact we are strengthened by the bonds of fellowship and friendship in the group and not burdened by the fear that we will soon again slump into our depression.[4] *(M45-46)*

■2.16 PLEASE COMMENT ON THE ABOVE STATEMENT AND WRITE OUT YOUR OWN PROGRAM FOR REGAINING SERENITY AND HOPE IN YOUR PERSONAL LIFE.

■2.17 List *eight* behaviors and/or thought patterns that will help you truly begin to believe that a power greater than yourself is restoring you to sanity!
■2.17 to ■2.17.8
■2.18 Please write down again how you have a different feeling about god now that you are working your 12 step program of recovery. Tell how this is happening in your life today!

THE DEPRESSED ANONYMOUS WORKBOOK

And now think about the following:

"Remember that an oak tree was once an acorn — recovery begins by taking one step at a time and accepting responsibility for moving from depression into peace and serenity."[5]

The Depressed Anonymous Statement of Belief #5

STEP THREE

"Made a decision to turn our will and our lives over to the care of God as we understood God. "

Step Three of Depressed Anonymous

Step three seems to stump a goodly number of persons who are moving through the steps one at a time. In the Depressed Anonymous manual we read that:

This decision to turn our lives over to god is one of the most important we will ever make in our lives. The more we surrender to his peace the more we will find our way...[1] **(M46)**

■3.1 Please comment on this statement. Have you ever turned your will and your life over to god before?

■3.2 Have you completely turned your will and/or life over to a professional, such as a doctor or counselor or other mental health professional?
In our program we learn that to surrender is not to lose but to win. This is a paradox.

■3.3 How do you relate to this statement where it says:
...This is the time to give up our will and say "God, you take it – I've had it! You do the leading now!" And you know, God will. You will begin to get more honest with yourself as you begin to look a little more closely at why you have been sad most of your life...[2] **(M46)**

■3.4 PLEASE COMMENT!
In your own life you may have understood god to be a fierce and tyrannical lawgiver who gives out only harsh punishments to those who disobey his laws and commandments. This god as we understood him is an important part of this workbook process because we can't move on into the step about discovery of our person till we have made up our mind to turn our life and our will since so far nothing has been able to remove the pain of our sadness. This is a big step for all of us who have learned that it is only safe to trust in ourselves rather than in someone else. Others always seem to let us down somehow.

Do you believe the following statement might apply to yourself?

THE DEPRESSED ANONYMOUS WORKBOOK

By daily prayer and meditation time we soon learn that the more frequent our contact is with the Higher Power, the more in touch this force will be in our lives and the more trust will you give to its leading...[3] **(M53)**

■3.5 How much would you say you are trusting of yourself?

■3.6 Do you allow your real feelings to emerge or are they pushed down so that you are unable to feel most of the time?

In our manual it states:

...These **"SUNSPOTS"** are meditation times where we can focus on all those pleasurable events, people, places or things that can make us feel happy. The trouble with most of us when we are depressed is that our whole life seems to go on in a deep pit inside an eighty foot hole and with an eight foot ladder...

Think upon these small "Sunspots" throughout the day and know that you are gradually coming into the light of a new day. Prepare a list of memories which at one time in your life were the cause of some joy or pleasure, and try to recreate that activity in your imagination as often as you can. At first all you might be able to do is just make a mental decision to do it even at the time you don't feel any particular pleasant emotion... Keep at it and with the continued encouragement of the group you will be able to recapture a little joy and peace...[4] **(M47-48)**

■3.7 Pretend that you are putting together a photo album of the happiest moments or most pleasant events of your life. Imagine they are still photos and that you place them in chronological order. When you feel sad you will then look through the album --one by one – and have a pleasant feeling take over your mind and heart. Now list these eight pictures and the subjects that they represent.

■3.7.1 to ■3.7.8
Our manual states that:
Control is an issue which all addicts of whatever substance, emotion or relationships have to look at sooner or later in their recovery...5 (M49)

■3.8 In what ways do you control others or allow others to control you? Do you allow your trapped feelings of depression to give you control over others in that they have to live with your manifestations of hopelessness.

These are quotes from Dorothy Rowe in her work breaking the Bonds:
■3.9 "What advantages do you get out of being depressed? It sounds strange to ask that question but is there truth in what it asks?

THE DEPRESSED ANONYMOUS WORKBOOK

■3.10 Whom are you protecting?

■3.11 Whom are you afraid to upset?

■3.12 What is it that you need to control?"

■3.13 How would you describe the way you usually relate to other people – controlling them or being dependent on them, or varying between the two? Or some other way?

■3.14 What changes do you need to make in yourself in order to get closer to other people?[6]

■3.15 Please discuss how the issue of being in control applies to you and how has this need kept you isolated and withdrawn and made to fall deeper into the pit of depression?

In step three we have to make a decision. We don't have to feel holy or extra nice but that we only have to make a decision – that is hard for someone who is depressed but it can be done. There is an old saying that goes like this: "Have a nice day unless you have made other plans."

I want to start to really begin to turn things over to the God of my understanding. In Depressed Anonymous we call this God our Higher Power.

As Bill W said:

"We realize we know only a little. God will constantly disclose more to you and to us. Ask him in your morning meditations what you can do each day for the man who is still sick. The answers will come, if your own house is in order.

But obviously you cannot transmit something you haven't got. See to it that your relationship with Him is right, and great events will come to pass for you and countless others. This is the great fact for us."[7]

And to the newcomer a caution is given:

Abandon yourself to God as you understand God. Admit your faults to Him and to your fellows. Clear away the wreckage of your past. Give freely of what you find and join us. We shall be with you in the fellowship of the spirit, and you will surely meet some of us as you trudge the road of happy destiny.

May God bless you and keep you – until then.

THE DEPRESSED ANONYMOUS WORKBOOK

■3.16 Do you feel that your relationship with God is right? How so and if not, why not? Please write out your thoughts below.

We discovered the best possible source of emotional stability to be God Himself. We found that dependence upon His perfect justice, forgiveness and love was healthy, and that it would work where nothing else would.

If we really depended upon God, we couldn't very well play God to our fellows, nor would we feel the urge to rely wholly on human protection and care.[9]

In the **Twelve Steps and Twelve Traditions** it states:

"But the moment our mental or emotional independence is in question, how differently we behave. How persistently we claim the right to decide all by ourselves just what we shall think and just how we shall act. Oh yes, we'll weigh the pros and cons of every problem. We'll listen politely to those who would advise us, but all the decisions are to be ours alone. Nobody is going to meddle with our personal independence in such matters. Besides, we think, there is no one we can surely trust. We are certain that our intelligence, backed by will power, can rightly control our inner lives and guarantee us success in the world we live in. This brave philosophy, wherein each man plays god, sounds good in the speaking, but it still has to meet the acid test. How well does it actually work? One good look in the mirror ought to be answer enough for any alcoholic.[10]

And again:

...In the first two steps we were engaged in reflection. We saw that we were powerless over alcohol, but we also perceived that faith of some kind, if only in A.A. itself, is possible to anyone. These conclusions did not require action: they required only acceptance.

Like all the remaining steps, Step three calls for affirmative action, for it is only by action that we can cut away the self-will which has always blocked the entry of God--or, if you like, a higher power --into our lives.[11]

And further it states:

Then it is explained that other steps of the A.A. program can be practiced with success only when Step Three is given a determined and persistent trial. This statement may surprise newcomers who have experienced nothing but constant deflation and a growing conviction that human will is of no value whatever. They have become persuaded, and rightly so, that many problems besides alcohol (depression) will not yield to a headlong assault powered by the individual alone.

THE DEPRESSED ANONYMOUS WORKBOOK

But now it appears that there are certain things which only the individual can do. All by himself, and in the light of his own circumstances, he needs to develop the quality of willingness. When he acquires willingness, he is the only who can make the decision to exert himself. Trying to do this is an act of his own will. All of the twelve steps require sustained and personal exertion to conform to their principles and so, we trust, to God's will....

...To all of us, this was most wonderful revelation; our whole trouble had been the misuse of will power. We had tried to bombard our problems with it instead of attempting to bring it into agreement with God's intention for us. To make this increasingly possible is the purpose of AA's twelve steps, and Step three opens the doors.[12]

■3.17 What three things today do you plan to do today so as to have a greater ability to turn your life and will over to the care of god as you understand him?

■3.18
List three...
■3.18.1
■3.18.2
■3.18.3
The manual says:
"With any addiction to an experience, be it alcohol, eating, gambling, smoking, and for us depression, we all know there is no "cheap grace" here in getting free of our dependency. Jim learned, in time and with frequent attendance at DA meetings, that the price of freedom from the uneasiness and hollow feelings he felt was every day to trust in the Higher Power and turn his sadness over to this god of his as he understood him."[13] **(M51)**

■3.19 Write down your response.
In the book As Bill Sees It, he comments that:
Perhaps one of the greatest rewards of meditation and prayer is the sense of belonging that comes to us. We no longer live in a completely hostile world. We are no longer lost and frightened and purposeless.
The moment we catch even a glimpse of God's will, the moment we begin to see truth, justice, and love as the real and eternal thing in life, we are no longer deeply disturbed by all the seeming evidence to the contrary that surrounds us in purely human affairs. We know that God lovingly watches over us. We know that when we turn to Him, all will be well with us, here and hereafter.[1]

■3.20 How has the daily practice of your prayer and meditation time brought you gradually to a belief that all in time will be well with you!

■3.21 What in the Depressed Anonymous meetings has brought you to an awareness that the god of your understanding wants to bring you out of depression?

Singleness of purpose

As Bill W says it:

"Our society (AA and or DA), therefore, will prudently cleave to its single purpose: the carrying of the message to the alcoholic (depressed) w h o still suffers. Let us resist the proud assumption that since God has enabled us to do well in one area we are destined to be a channel of saving grace for everybody."[15]

One thing the Higher Power accomplishes for any of us is the freedom of being in His will. By turning your life and your will over to a Higher Power you can make a new beginning, you get a new start, you can forgive yourself for all the times you thought you needed to be perfect...[16]

■3.22 Please write out from this point on how your desire and your decision to be a survivor and no longer a victim of depression is to be worked out in your personal life.

We lose the fear of making decisions, great and small, as we realize that should our c h o i c e prove wrong we can, we will learn from the experience. Should our decision be the right one, we can thank God for giving us the courage and the grace that caused us so to act.[17]

Our **Depressed Anonymous** manual reads:

God, I offer myself to thee -- to build with me and to do with me as thou wilt. Relieve me o f the bondage of self, that I may better do thy will. Take away my difficulties, that transcendence over them may bear witness to those I would help of Thy Power, Thy Love, and Thy way of life. May I do Thy will always.[18] **(M52)**

THE DEPRESSED ANONYMOUS WORKBOOK

■3.23 List some ways that you intend to become more attuned to God's will as you struggle to free yourself from depression? What will it take, as you perceive it, to rid yourself from the pain of your depression?"

"The greatest gift that can come to anybody is a spiritual awakening.[19]

STEP FOUR

"Made a searching and fearless moral inventory of ourselves."

<u>The Fourth Step of Depressed Anonymous.</u>

Step four is the beginning of getting a start on looking at our lives. Its focus is on the present and continues the work of the first three steps. Now that I have admitted that I need help and that only a power greater than myself can restore me to sanity am I ready to turn my will and my life over to the care of God as I understand him. What is that I need to change in my life in order to feel differently? How is the changing going to make a difference on the way that I perceive my world, my relationships and myself. Where do I start in this process of recovery? The when is definitely now in the present. I have already spent a good amount of time wishing to change the way I feel and live my life. I also have contemplated how much differently I needed to feel. I find that taking the 4th step is the actual preparation for the change that I am bent on accomplishing.

Step four is about taking action and getting on top of how I need to change. Then comes the remainder of the steps.

GETTING STARTED AND GETTING FIRST THINGS FIRST!

1. FIRST READ THE WHOILE DOCUMENT AT YOUR OWN PACE.

2. SPEND QUALITY TIME ANSWERING EACH QUESTION.

3. GET A NOTEPAD AND WRITE DOWN YOUR RESPONES TO EACH QUESTION.

4. KNOW THAT THE FOURTH STEP IS NOT A BLAMIMG OURSELVES FOR OUR SADNESS.

MORAL: A DEFINITION

■ 1. Relating to dealing with, or capable of making the distinction between right and wrong, in conduct. 2. Serving to teach, or in accordance with the principles of right and wrong. 3. Good or right in conduct or character....

Moral implies conformity with the generally accepted standards of goodness or rightness in conduct, sometimes, specifically, in sexual conduct [a moral person]; ethical implies conformity with an elaborated code of moral principles, sometimes specifically., with the code of a particular profession [an ethical lawyer] virtuous implies a morally excellent character, connoting justice, integrity, and often, specifically chastity. (Source: *WEBSTER'S NEW WORLD DICTIONARY, 1989.*)

When I speak of the 4th step of **DEPRESSED ANONYMOUS** this means that we are now ready to make a moral and fearless inventory of our lives. It also means that we are ready for action and choose to change the way we live out our daily life. Fearless means brave and courageous.

By now, most of us are aware that because of our depression our lives are unmanageable and out of control. They are out of control to such an extent that we may have even thought about ending our lives.

We have admitted that there is a power out there that is greater than ourselves and that we are willing to turn our minds and our wills over to the care of God as we understand God.

If we just take a little time, look at the way we talk to ourselves we may discover the reason for our depression. So often we turn and run when the old feelings of sadness appear in front of us. What we want to try and do now is to look the beast in the face and deal with it.

Just let's say that you always took path A home from work every day. You passed the same old signs, the same old buildings, the same old malls – you feel you could almost drive home with your eyes closed. This is of course boring and also deadening to our thinking processes as we do everything out of habit. The saying is true that we are creatures of habit. But let's just say that there is a detour along our old familiar path – we become disoriented – we become confused – we say to ourselves – where am I? Now where do I go? Good questions.

Since we may presently be depressed and feeling in that deep dark pit of depression we may decide that we don't have anything to gain by reading on at this point in our discussion. But I know and you know that you want out of the darkness. Many depressions just lift by themselves but many don't and because of

THE DEPRESSED ANONYMOUS WORKBOOK

the way we were brought up as children many of the negative ways we think about ourselves have been with us since childhood. Old ideas about ourselves die hard and so do old impressions from the early days of life.

Our personal attachment to feeling isolated, alone and worthless is like a road from which we can't exit. Our attachment to our sadness is a comfort in a strange sort of way – almost like the person who is addicted or attached to a chemical, behavior, way of thinking, or even a person.

But we have figured out that even though my path home is very predictable it is still a path that is gradually incapacitating my ability to keep a focus on any hopeful outcome.

Working the 4th step is like coming home a different route. It is a path that is filled with signposts that point us in a different direction than where we are used to going. And for many of us this is the first time that we are really intent upon taking a good hard look at who we are. This taking inventory of ourselves has much to do with our loving ourselves and making ourselves open to a new path and feeling different.

To actually get started on working a good fourth step we need first of all to sit down, get a pen or pencil and begin to ask ourselves some questions. As soon as the answers come we then write these down and begin our inventory. It's always best to look at ourselves through the black and white characters that translate our thoughts and feelings down on paper. Remember this inventory is about strengths as well as our character defects and character defects are ways of thinking, feeling, behaving that keep us isolated and in pain. Let's not get out of balance here and think that this is a lynching party for ourselves. The inventory is not to make us feel bad but is to help us understand what is keeping us in the pit of sadness.

Writing down information about oneself will help you see possibly for the first time what keeps you feeling sad. Many persons depressed understand what is making them feel sad by sitting down, grabbing a pencil, and trying to get in touch with what is making them feel abandoned, lost or hurting. Sometimes just making an effort day after day to understand our sadness will get you in touch with the reason for the depression and it may lift immediately and won't reappear for a few days. The more one keeps at this process of eliminating fears and anxieties the more your days will be happier and less filled with despair. The more you fight fear the more it persists. What you resist persists. Admit and accept your depression and find it not to be the fearful demon that we suspected.

THE DEPRESSED ANONYMOUS WORKBOOK

■4.1 WRITE DOWN WHAT HAPPENS TO YOU WHEN YOU ARE DEPRESSED.
Depression can actually be a way of taking care of ourselves. It can be protection, solace, and comfort. We can view it like a soft blanket we can wrap up in.

It's no accident that when people get depressed they often go to bed and eat. We attempt to return to a sort of infant state. We reduce the world to a simple sleep and eat state. Get into a warm place; get the tummy full of food. We want to be little and taken care of.

This slows us down and gives us time to find the line between denying ourselves and indulging ourselves. It helps us discover what we really need.[1]

FUN? WHEN WAS THE LAST TIME YOU HAD SOME?

■4.2 Explore your beliefs. Have you had fun lately? Write down and list all the enjoyable activities that you engaged in this last week?

■4.3 List as many pleasant activities that you can remember before you became depressed? Attempt to do at least one of these old friends once a day. Keep track of how well you do.

Doing this thorough inventory is an action step that promises to begin freeing up years of accumulated grief, hurt and pain. Only by getting started and doing something can we get the juices started and continue to stay motivated to attempt change. We find that our motivation builds the more we force ourselves to take action!

When we finally are prepared to make our fourth step what we are doing *is* stopping the continued drifting through life and living within the narrow confines of a habituated way of thinking about ourselves. We are going to stop the drift! We are going to learn how to become conscious of the way we have been absentmindedly shortchanging ourselves and our life. We are about to do this inventory because we know there is something better out there for me than what I have now. The 4th step is my new beginning. Things will begin to change for me as I gradually take one negative brick out of the wall that keeps me isolated from the rest of the world.

READ WITH CARE THE FOLLOWING!!!

THE DEPRESSED ANONYMOUS WORKBOOK

Step four is a critical step if we want to begin the journey toward wholeness, peace and having good feelings about having good feelings about ourselves. But if we want to stay in the pit of sadness then the belief that we are worthless and not quit good enough will definitely limit our awareness of what we can become and what we can do for ourselves. I believe a lot of our difficulties have their roots in our need to be perfect and to do things the way others expect. It's as though we have to take care of their needs before our own. Significant persons from our past have promoted the belief that for me to be acceptable I had to do things their way and their way alone. I had to please them or I might be abandoned and left alone forever. This in itself is a frightening situation for any of us. I needed continually to attempt to be someone other than myself. I constantly was filled with a sadness, as I never felt I could measure up to what others wanted me to do or be. My whole life was graded on what others thought I should be. Good was never good enough and so I continued to test the limits in an effort to excel but the limits were never clearly marked out. I sensed that somehow I couldn't ever measure up to others expectations and that made me feel ashamed of myself. Not only did I feel guilt but I also felt ashamed of myself. Not only did I feel guilt but I also felt ashamed - ashamed that my inadequacies would be exposed for everyone to see and ridicule. My constant fear was that others would see how bad I really was.[2] **(M54).**

■4.4 The moral and fearless inventory is not going to leave one rock unturned as I begin to gather evidence that I need to begin anew and try and live one day at a time. I will learn how to stop and listen to the words I often say to myself when I feel myself spiraling down into the pit of depression. If I can do this day after day, and only one day at a time I know that there will be hope for me. If I have ever had one good day in my life I know that I am about to have another.

■4.5 How do you see yourself in this statement from the manual?

The first immutable belief, according to Dorothy Rowe, that many depressed hold onto, like the inspired words from God, is the belief that no matter how good and nice I appear to be, I am really bad, evil, valueless, unacceptable to myself and to others.[3] **(M54)**

With the 4th step I am finally willing to get on with taking a deeper look at me and to check out to see what makes up this fear that seems to be hanging over my head like a dark and deadly cloud.

THE DEPRESSED ANONYMOUS WORKBOOK

As it says in the **Twelve and Twelve:**

Step four is our vigorous and painstaking effort to discover what these liabilities in e a c h of us have been. By discovering what our emotional deformities are, we can move toward their correction. Without a willing and persistent effort to do this, there can be little sobriety or contentment for us. Without a searching and fearless moral inventory, most of us have found that the faith which really works in daily living is still out of reach.[4]

And again:

There is a direct linkage among self-examination, meditation and prayer. Taken separately, these practices can bring much relief and benefit. But when they are logically related and interwoven, the result is an unshakable foundation for life.[5]

By our daily conscious contact with God as we understand him I believe that my daily efforts at listening to my Higher Power's word will help me focus in on where I need to change. I hope that my depression will always be examined the moment I feel down and blue for no apparent reason. If I slow down, take a pencil and write what I have been thinking of late I do believe that my sadness will slowly evaporate --much like the early morning fog.

I exorcise my fears, guilt and resentments by getting them down on paper in front of me.

■4.6 Get the facts about ourselves. Does your mind and body respond in certain predictable ways? You will find you need life to be certain and predictable because if life was unpredictable then life would be filled with risks. With feeling depressed you know what you have. With life the way you have it now you have no hope of ever feeling differently because you are afraid to risk living with uncertainty!

■4.7 After taking responsibility for ourselves and taking our personal inventory -- and that on a daily basis -- we can begin to feel differently and new horizons of hope will open up before us.

■4.8 Reflections about our life can lead us out of our depression by enabling us to develop new strategies for coping with old beliefs that we once held about ourselves.

If our images of God fluctuate between dictator, judge and kind friend our devotion today may ebb and flow and our affection may be blocked by anger with God's powerlessness. Our fears of what God might ask of us (some will read: require, demand of us) may overwhelm us. One way to explore our fear or our embarrassment about loving God is to explore the freedom, spontaneity, playfulness with which we love some of our favorite human beings. Whom do you currently love best in all the world? Think of that person in concrete detail and let your feelings for that person arise. Do you feel afraid? Embarrassed? Guarded? Why or why not?

■4.9 PLEASE WRITE DOWN YOUR RESPONSES TO THESE QUESTIONS. GETTING YOUR HISTORY RIGHT – GETTING STARTED. CHECK OFF THE ONES THAT YOU WANT TO ANSWER

After each question you will see these letters S/R. They are the signs that mean that you are to = STOP AND REFLECT, (S/R).

■4.10 Do you remember the first time you were able to feel the loss of someone you love? (S/R)

■4.11 List all those significant people who died before you were ten years old. What can you remember about their funerals? Stop and reflect (S/R)

■4.12 Can you remember your own feelings at the time of the wake or the funeral? (S/R)

■4.13 Have I allowed myself to grieve and mourn the loss of loved ones in the past or have I repressed these emotions of loss, sadness and separation? (S/R)

■4.14 Can you remember losing a beloved pet or an animal that you loved as a child? (S/R)

■4.15 Am I still mad about a painful situation in my past life? (S/R)

■4.16 Do I still feel guilty about something that I did years ago and never told anyone about? (S/R)

■4.17 Do I still hold resentments about something or someone? (S/R) Am I still mad at Dad or Mom for divorcing and causing myself to feel abandoned or lost? (S/R)

■4.18 Am I angry with God? Write down some of the reasons that you have for being angry with God? Do you feel that some of his representatives treated you unfairly? Can you think of some of the particular instances where you feel you were mistreated? (S/R)

■4.19 Do I think that God won't forgive me for a past action of mine? (S/R)

■4.20 Do I have trouble trusting GOD? S/R Do I believe that God has my best interests at heart? (S/R)

■4.21 Do I find that I likewise have trouble trusting others who share my life with me? (S/R)

■4.22 What type of feeling did I receive about God when I was growing up? (S/R)Did my parents, teachers, Bible school teachers present God as a friend or as a harsh parent? (S/R)

■4.23 Have you ever felt God's presence in your life? (S/R)

■4.24 Write down the times that you felt God's presence especially close to you. (S/R)

■4.25 Do you believe that God is always looking for punish you? *S/R*

FAMILY OF ORIGIN

In order to make a good inventory I need to go to my roots and discover how I came to be the person that I am today. As the saying goes, "We are our parents."

When we were small we "swallowed" our parents, meaning "swallowed" their main personality characteristics. Even today parents, grandparents, a stepparent, or guardian are all now part of our personality – for good or for ill. For myself to escape from my depression I need to discover how I might have received certain messages about myself from these adults who surrounded me as a helpless infant and child. All of us have received messages as children – some helpful and others not so helpful. Some messages directed toward us might have made us feel worthless because we got the message that we could never do anything to please others.

■4.26 How was your relationship with your Father's parents? How about your relationship with your Mother's parents? Write down the positive memories of your childhood as they relate to your grandparents? (S/R)

■4.27 Was there alcoholism or depression in your family background? We know that children of alcoholic parents have troubles of their own as they grow older. Alcoholic families are usually abusive and chaotic. The life of a child growing up in such a dysfunctional family usually is a frightening experience. (*S/R*)

THE DEPRESSED ANONYMOUS WORKBOOK

■4.28 Did you ever have a birthday party as you were growing up? Write down the feelings you can remember about those occasions. (S/R)

■4.29 Do you remember much of your childhood or are there gaps in your memory about certain periods of your childhood? (S/R)

■4.30 Was your mother or father the more strict? (S/R)

■4.31 Were you allowed to express your feelings as a child? (S/R)

■NOW TAKE SOME TIME AND GO BACK AND WRITE OUT IN MORE DETAIL THE QUESTIONS THAT YOU CHECKED? FINISHED? PROCEED

RESENTMENTS
■4.32 The BIG BOOK OF AA SAYS

That on our grudge list we set opposite each name our injuries. Was it our self-esteem, our security, our ambitions, our personal feelings, our sexual relations, which had been interfered with?

Example

I'm Resentful at	The Cause	Affects
■1. Mr. Jones	He may get my job at the office	Self-esteem (Fear)
■2. Mrs. Jones	She's a nut – she snubbed me	Personal relationship
■3. Myself	I feel I'm a failure	My attitudes (Anxiety)
■4. Parents	Never praised me	Self-esteem (Anger)

■4.33 Please continue with your own personal list and gradually allow yourself who and what you might find yourself resenting while digging out the various causes and then listing below the various ways these affect your moods.

...We asked ourselves why we were angry. In most cases it was found that our self-esteem, our pocketbooks, our personal relationships, (including sex) were hurt or threatened. So we were sore. We were "burned up."[6]

THE DEPRESSED ANONYMOUS WORKBOOK

CHECK ANY OR ALL THAT MAY APPLY TO YOU!

_____NO MATTER HOW GOOD AND NICE I APPEAR TO BE, I AM REALLY BAD, EVIL, VALUELESS, UNACCEPTABLE TO MYSELF AND OTHERS.[7]

■4.34 Please write down how this belief applies to you.

_____OTHER PEOPLE ARE SUCH THAT I MUST FEAR, HATE AND ENVY THEM.

■4.35 Please write down how this belief applies to you.

_____LIFE IS TERRIABLE AND DEATH IS WORSE.

■4.36 Please write down how this belief applies to you.

_____ONLY BAD THINGS HAPPENED TO ME IN THE PAST AND ONLY BAD THINGS WILL HAPPEN TO ME IN THE FUTURE.

■4.37 Please write down how this belief applies to you.

_____ANGER IS EVIL.

■4.38 Please write down how this belief applies to you.

_____MUST NEVER FORGIVE ANYONE, LEAST OF ALL MYSELF.

■4.39 Please write down how this belief applies to you.

THE SIX STATEMENTS ABOVE ARE QUOTED FROM: DEPRESSION: THE WAY OUT OF THE PRISON AUTHORED BY DR. DOROTHY ROWE.

THESE AFOREMENTIONED ARE THE SIX MAIN INGREDIENTS OF DEPRESSION. THESE BELIEFS TENACIOUSLY HELD; IMPRISON THE DEPRESSED UNTIL THAT DAY WHEN THEY MAKE A DECISION TO REMOVE THE BARS.

■4.40 NOW SPEND SOME QUALITY TIME WRITING DOWN HOW ANY OR ALL OF THESE SIX BELIEFS APPLY TO YOU AND YOUR LIFE, BOTH PAST AND PRESENT.

FINISHED? PLEASE PROCEED:

We turned back to the list, for it hid the key to the future. We were prepared to look at it from an entirely different angle. We began to see the world and its people really dominated us. In that state, the wrong doing of others, fancied or real, had power to actually kill.... Referring to our list again. Putting out of our minds the wrongs others had done, we resolutely looked for our own mistakes. Where had we been, selfish, dishonest, self-seeking and frightened? Though a situation had not been entirely our fault, we tried to disregard the other person involved entirely. Where we to blame? The inventory was ours, not the other person's. When we saw our faults we listed them. We placed them before us in black and white. We admitted our wrongs honestly and we were willing to set these matters straight.

Notice that the word "fear" is bracketed alongside the difficulties with Mr. Brown, Mrs. Jones, the employer, and the wife. This short word touches about every aspect of our lives...

We reviewed our fears thoroughly. We put them on paper, even though we had no resentment in connection with them. We asked ourselves why we had them. Wasn't it because self-reliance failed us? Self-reliance was good as far as it went, but it didn't go far enough. Some of us once had great self-confidence, but it didn't fully solve the fear problem, or any other...

We reviewed our own conduct over the years past. Where had we been selfish, dishonest, or inconsiderate? Whom had we hurt? Did we unjustifiably arouse jealousy, suspicion or bitterness? Where were we at fault, what should we have done instead? We got this all down on paper and looked at it.[8]

Resentment means hanging onto a feeling (to re-feel) of ill will toward that person or persons who have hurt us. We keep going over in our minds the wrongs done to us by another. In fact resentments are the key in our getting ourselves depressed. Many times r e s e n t m e n t is an anger that has been turned inward. Since anger is a big part of our depression let's examine it for what it is.

ANGER WORKSHOP
CHECKLIST FOR HIDDEN ANGER

If we have any unexpected fault, it is hiding our own anger from ourselves. Here is a checklist to help you determine if you are hiding your anger from yourself. Any of these is usually a sign of hidden unexpected anger.

1. Procrastination in the completion of imposed tasks
2. Perpetual or habitual lateness
3. A liking for sadistic or ironic humor
4. Overly polite, constant cheerfulness, attitude of "grin and bear it."
5. Frequent sighing
6. Sarcasm, cynicism or flippancy in conversation
7. Smiling while hurting
8. Frequent disturbing or frightening dreams
9. Over controlled monotone speaking voice
10. Difficulty in getting to sleep or sleeping through the night
11. Boredom
12. Slowing down of movements

13. Getting tired more easily than usual
14. Excessive irritability over trifles
15. Getting drowsy at inappropriate times
16. Sleeping more than usual
17. Waking up tired rather than rested or refreshed
18. Clenched jaws – especially while sleeping
19. Facial tics, spasmodic foot movements, habitual fist clenching and similar repeated acts done unintentionally or unaware
20. Grinding of teeth– especially while sleeping
21. Chronically stiff neck or shoulder muscles
22. Chronic depression – extended periods of feelings down for no reason
23. Stomach ulcers/gastrointestinal problems

■4.41 NOW OF THE 23 ITEMS LISTED ABOVE, PLEASE CHECK OFF THE ONES THAT APPLY TO YOU. WRITE DOWN IF ANY OF THESE CHECKED ITEMS HAVE ANYTIDNG TO DO WITH YOUR SADDING YOURSELF?

Because you are unaware of being angry does not mean that you are not angry. It is the anger you are unaware of which can do the most damage to you and to your relationships with other people, since it does get expressed, but in appropriate ways. Freud once likened anger to the smoke in an old fashioned wood burning stove. The normal avenue for discharge of the smoke is up the flue and out the chimney; if the normal avenue is blocked, the smoke will leak out the stove in unintended ways...around the door, through the grate, etc., choking everyone in the room. If all avenues of escape are blocked, the fire goes out and the stove ceases to function. Likewise, the normal human expression of anger is gross physical movement and/or loud vocalization; watch a red-faced hungry infant sometime. We learn to "be nice," which means (among other things) hiding "bad" feelings. By adulthood, even verbal expression is curtailed, since a civilized person is expected to be "civil." Thus, expression is stifled, and to protect ourselves from the unbearable burden of continually unexpressed "bad" feelings, we go to the next step and convince ourselves that we are not angry, even when we are. Such self-deception is seldom completely successful and the blocked anger "leaks out" in inappropriate ways, some of which are listed above.[9]

WHAT AM I FEELING?
ANGER   HOSTILITY   AGGRESSION

Anger: An emotion that says "something is wrong." it can be expressed to tell others about your personal limits, values, rules, and boundaries. The respectful expression of anger is an important way to educate others about how their behavior affects you. It can result in mutual respect between you and another person.

Hostility: An attitude that contributes to the violation of another person's right's, values, rules, or boundaries. This attitude can include ruminating or brooding about another person's real or perceived injustices toward you and ways that you can "get even" with him/her. This attitude leads to feelings of powerlessness. It can often lead to aggression or withdrawal as a way to punish others.

Aggression: A behavior, acted on with the intent to harm others, either physically or emotionally for real or imagined "wrongs" done to you. This behavior always results in disrespect for yourself and the other person. It creates distance between you rather that brining you closer

LEARNING HOW TO EXPRESS ANGER RESPECTFULLY

1. Admit your anger. Accept that you are angry. Shouting "I am not angry!" at the other person only escalates you more. It can be safe and growth producing to acknowledge that you are angry.
2. Take a "time out" to cool down if you need it. Learning to deal respectfully and constructively with you anger takes time and practice.
3. Identify the source of your anger (look for your primary feelings). Make sure you perceived what happened correctly. Ask yourself questions like: "What is my negative self-talk?" Am I dealing only with this issue at hand or are there other stressors that have already escalated me before this?" "Am I looking for a reason to blow up?"
4. Separate the energy of your anger (pent-up feelings inside you seeking release) from the issue your anger is about (the condition, idea, event, or person you feel angry at).
5. Decide how and when you will express your anger.
6. Talk to the other person involved with your anger. Share your anger and any primary feelings you can identify in an open, direct, and respectful way.

7. Make "I" statements. Take responsibility for your own feelings. Resist the temptation to blame someone else for "making you" feel angry.

8. Listen closely to the other's point of view. Recognize and accept their view may be quite different from yours. Remember that they have right to their perspective and feelings.

9. Get in touch with your expectations and your intentions in sharing your anger.

The purpose is not to "win" the argument (or discussion) or to make the other person agree with your point of view. Rather, it is an opportunity to give both of you a time to express feelings. Also, explore a l t e r n a t i v e s such as compromising, "Agreeing to disagree," or table the discussion until another time.[10]

● ●

THE FOLLOWING IS A CHECKLIST OF CHARACTER DEFECTS/SHORTCOMINGS THAT I MIGHT APPLY TO MYSELF.

●PROCRASTINATION

Because I might make a mistake I fail to take any initiative in correcting the course I am on in my life and so I do nothing to help myself feel differently. Sometimes I fail to take action for myself because I am afraid that I might likewise have to change the way I think and feel about my life.

■4.42 WRITE DOWN HOW YOU MIGHT PROCRASTINATE"

●NOT TRUSTING OTHERS

One of the reasons the world looks so bad when we are depressed is that we feel so bad about ourselves and we can't ever trust ourselves to feel good about ourselves, our world or our future. So it would appear that it is difficult to go and trust others.

■4.43 How would you describe the way you usually relate to other people - controlling them, being dependent on them, or varying between the two or some other way?

What changes do you need to make in yourself in order to get closer to other people?

Now that you have indicated the items that apply to your life, as far as you can remember DIALOGUE WITHIN YOURSELF how you came to believe these truths and how you have incorporated it or them into your everyday life. Also can you see how each of these beliefs have helped you depress yourself or have kept yourself depressed?

●We're there family secrets that weren't allowed to be talked about outside my home? Secrets that we hold about ourselves could be some of the following.

    a. My depression addiction; alcoholism in the family

    b. I was sexually abused/physically abused

c. I was perceived as a failure in life.

d. Mental problems in the family

e. Incestuous relationships in one's own family.

■4.44 Did we ever see our parents showing affection for each other. Did we experience our parents fighting on a regular basis? *S/R*

■4.45 Did we fear as youngsters that our Mother and Father would leave us? How did that make you feel? Does someone you love leaving you today remind you of that past fear? *S/R*

■4.46 if our parents did divorce did we blame ourselves for the divorce even though we know now that we were not the cause of the divorce? *S/R*

Significant persons from our past have promoted the belief that for me to be acceptable I had to do things their way and their way alone. I had to please him or I might be abandoned and left alone forever[11] (**M54**)

HERE IS ANOTHER LIST OF SOME OF THE SHORTCOMINGS WE NEED TO EXAMINE IF WE ARE TO CHANGE SO THAT WE MAY LIVE WITH SOME SERENITY. EACH OF THE WORDS AND PHRASES LISTED BELOW CAN BE SEEN AS A BRICK IN THE WALL THAT BLOCK'S ONE'S CONTINUED RECOVERY FROM DEPRESSION. ON THE LINES BEFORE EACH EXPRESSION RATE THE EXTENT TO WHICH EACH OF THESE HAS PLAYED A KEY ROLE IN THE WAY YOU HAVE CONSTRUCTED YOUR WORLD – YOUR REALITY.

■ Place a 1 through 5 to indicate the importance in your life of each of the following: #1 BEING THE LOWEST INFLUENCE AND # 5 BEING THE GREATEST.

_____PAST HURTS
_____ANGER
_____GUILT
_____BITTERNESS
_____BURNOUT FEAR
_____BOREDOM
_____STRESS

THE DEPRESSED ANONYMOUS WORKBOOK

_____WORKAHOLISM
_____ANXIETY
_____PESSIMISM
_____RIGIDITY
_____AVOIDANCE
_____DWELLING IN PAST
_____WORRY WART
_____RESENTMENTS
_____COMPULSION TO REPEAT
_____NEGATIVE THOUGHTS
_____RUMINNATING OVER LOSSES
_____MAD AT GOD
_____PERFECRTIONIST
_____INDECISIVENESS
_____SELF-DOUBTS
_____ALL OR NOTHING THINKING
_____AVOIDANCE OF INTIMACY
_____PEOPLE PLEASING
_____PESSIMISM TOWARD SELF
_____LACK OF FEELING COMPETENT
_____FEELING UNCONNECTED TO THE WORLD
_____FEELING SMALL AND WANTING TO HIDE
_____LOSS OF AN IDENTITY
_____ANGER WITH GOD AS YOU UNDERSTAND GOD
_____PASSIVITY
_____HOSTILITY TOWARD OTHERS
_____BLAMING EVERYONE ELSE FOR OUR PROBLEMS
_____GULIT OVER REAL OR IMAGINED SINS COMMITED BY
OURSELVES
_____FEELING OURSELVES FAILURES
_____FEELING I'M A MISTAKE
_____WANTING TO CONTROL OTHERS
_____SELF-PITTY
_____RESENT OTHERS
_____LAZINESS
_____FEAR OF MAKING MISTAKES
_____DENIAL THAT I AM RESPONIBLE FOR MY DEPRESSION
_____FEARS
_____NON-ASSERTIVENESS

THE DEPRESSED ANONYMOUS WORKBOOK

■4.47 Now pick out **seven** of the above list that you have ranked with your highest number and write a few sentences about how these characteristics have caused you to live life less fully or even to cause you to depress yourself.

■4.47.1 to ■4.47.7

WRITE DOWN YOUR OWN REACTIONS TO THE EXAMPLES BELOW. THESE BELIEFS MAY KEEP YOU DEPRESSED!

The following are paraphrased from a work by Albert Ellis, <u>REASON AND EMOTION IN PSYCHOTHERAPY</u>. 1962, Lyle Stuart, NY.[12]

{The comments following are taken from Thinking. Changing. Rearranging: Improving Self-esteem in young people.   Jill Anderson, Timberline Press, Eugene, OR 97401, Pages 51, 52. [13]}

■4.48.1 That it is a dire necessity for an adult human being to be loved by virtually every other significant person in his (her) community!
  Comment on this response:

■4.48.2 Everybody doesn't have to love me or even like me. I don't necessarily like everybody I know, so why should everybody else like me? I enjoy being liked and being loved, but if somebody doesn't like me, I will still be OK., and still feel like I am an OK person...

■4.48.3 The idea that one should be thoroughly competent and achieving in all possible respects if one is to consider him or herself worthwhile.
  Comment on this response:

■4.48.4 It is O.K. to make a mistake. Making mistakes is something we all do, and I am still a fine and worthwhile person when I make mistakes. There is no reason for me to get upset when I make a mistake...I will accept mistakes in myself and also mistakes that others make.

■4.48.5 The idea that it is awful and catastrophic when things are not the way one would very much like them to be.

■4.48.5B I know that things are hardly as bad as they seem.

■4.48.6 The idea that certain people are wicked, bad or evil, and that they should be punished for their evil ways.
Please comment on the following:

THE DEPRESSED ANONYMOUS WORKBOOK

■4.48.7 People who do things I don't like are not necessarily bad people. They should not necessarily be punished just because I don't like what they do or did. There is no reason why another person should be the way I want them to be, and there is no reason why I should be the way somebody else wants me to be....

■4.48.8 The idea that human unhappiness is externally caused, and that people have little or no ability to control their sorrows or disturbances.
Please comment on the following:

■4.48.9 I will survive if things are different than what I want them to be. I can accept things the way they are, accept people the way they are, and accept myself the way I am.
There is no reason to get upset if I can't change things to fit my ideas of how they ought to be....

■4.48.10 The idea that if something is, or may be, dangerous or fearsome, that one should terribly concerned about it and dwell upon the possibility of its occurring.
Please comment on the following:

■4.48.11 I don't need to watch out for things to go wrong. Things usually go just fine, and when they don't, I can handle it. I don't have to waste my energy worrying...

■4.48.12 The idea that it is easier to avoid than to face certain of life's difficulties. Please comment on the following:

■4.48.13 I can. Even though I may be faced with difficult tasks, it is better to try than to avoid them. Avoiding a task does not give me any opportunities for success or joy, but trying does. Things worth having are worth the effort. I might not be able to do everything, but I can do something.

■4.48.14 The idea that one should be dependent on others and need someone stronger than oneself on whom to rely.
Please respond to the following:

THE DEPRESSED ANONYMOUS WORKBOOK

■4.48.15 I don't need someone else to take care of my problems. I am capable. I can take care of myself. I can make decisions for myself... I can think for myself. I don't have to depend on somebody else to take care of me.

■4.48.16 The idea that one's past history is an all important determiner of one's present behavior, and that because something once strongly influenced one's life it should indefinitely have a similar impact.
Please comment on the following:

■4.48.17 I can change. I don't have to be a certain way because of what has happened in the past. Every day is a new day. It's silly to think I can't help being the way I am. Of course I can.

■4.48.18 The idea that one should be quite upset over other people's problems and disturbances.
Please comment on the following:

■4.48.19 I can't solve other people's problems for them. I don't have to take on other people's problems as if they were my own. I don't need to change other people, or fix up their lives. They are capable and can take care of themselves, and can solve their own problems.

NOW COMPLETE THE FOLLOWING LIST ABOUT YOURSELF
■4.49 I take pride in the following character strengths that I find in myself

■4.49.1
■4.49.2
■4.49.3
■4.49.4
■4.49.5
■4.49.6
■4.49.7
■4.49.8 and so on. (Write in Notebook)
■4.50 List the five most important people in your life that you feel you must please
■4.50.1
■4.50.2
■4.50.3
■4.50.4
■4.50.5

■4.51 Please list why you must please them and what would happen if you didn't please them?

Has depression distorted us from the truths of life, namely, that life is to be lived with hope and serenity. Nursing along a good habit can in time wean us from old and debilitating habits of thought and behavior. We want to daily fill our day with the gratitude that we are indeed getting better and that the trust we have is indeed placed in the Higher Power.

In order for us to escape depression we need to begin to be aware of the process of how people change. That process for change is of the nature of a spiral instead of a straight line. In other words, now that we are willing to risk feeling differently we have been gearing up to improve our situation. In other words we are making a very important decision right now about our lives.

1. Awareness Stage: We become conscious that we can't go on feeling the way we do. Something has to give.
2. Motivating Stage: I am going to prepare myself for needed changes in my thinking, acting and feeling.
3. Doing Stage: I am going to take charge and be responsible for positive changes that have to be made by me if I am to feel differently.
4. Maintaining Stage: I will continue to seek out and sustain my recovery with people, concepts and my personal working of the 12 step program for recovery.

■4.52 Now apply these four stages which serve as antidotes to our character defects and which cause us to stay imprisoned in our prison of depression.
Proceed and take any of those items on which you scored a five on pages 15 and 16 and use them in the formula of the four stages that have just been given. But first let's examine the following character defect according to our formula.

THE CHARACTER DEFECT IS
BLAMING.

(1) AWARE. Now that I have admitted I am powerless over my depression and that it serves no purpose to blame myself for my depression and bashing myself with daily reminders how bad and unacceptable I am. And now I am: (1)

AWARE of my need to discover what there is about myself that I do find acceptable, good and wholesome?

(2) I am MOTIVATING myself now that I am aware how I have depressed myself by the faulty beliefs that I have held about myself over the past years. I now know that part of the way I feel is due to the way I automatically talk to myself throughout the day. Without ever being conscious of it I now realize that my feelings about myself are very negative and emotion laden.

(3) DOING. I intend today to replace all negative statements that I make about in my head and replace them with positive statements --positive affirmations. I am 'going to alert myself -- like a red flag waving -- every time I call myself stupid or put myself down mentally. I will use affirmations such as I will build a new life. I am strong. I have the courage to go through this experience. I no longer blame myself or others for my sadness. I do not have to wait for someone to make me feel differently. I can do it myself.

(4) MAINTAINING I am very hopeful that I can feel differently just today, for this 24 hour period. I am going to tolerate my imperfectness while at the same time refusing to feel sorry for myself. I am going to make myself accountable for how I feel-- not blame it on another, the weather, parents or whatever.

THE CHARACTER DEFECT IS BEING VICTIM

EXAMPLE

(1) AWARE. I am learning through my program that as long as I blame everyone for the way I feel I will never improve or feel differently. I am now becoming conscious that I got myself depressed and now I am going to have to do something about it. I am not blaming myself for being depressed --that's counterproductive – but being conscious that I am depressed I am going to take full responsibility for getting out of it. I don't have to feel this way!

(2) MOTIVATING. I am making plans to check out the way I think-- the faulty patterns of automatic thinking that I have fallen into over my past life. I am going to see myself as a survivor as I live one day at a time and begin living with hope.

(3) DOING. Every day I am going to do something good and pleasant for myself. I am going to take mastery over my life by setting small goals one day at a time for feeling different. I am going to spend some time every day making conscious contact with the god of my understanding and pray that I might have knowledge of God's will for me and have the power to carry it out.

(4) MAINTAINING. I know there is no "cheap grace" in getting free from my depression. I also believe in having gratitude in that I have this spiritual program of recovery to continue my exit from the despair of depression. In order to sustain my healing I will take responsibility for all my words, thoughts and actions. I now believe that if my world is to change then it is up to me to change it. My Higher Power and myself are coworkers in my feeling whole and serene!

THE CHARACTER DEFECT IS ANXIETY.

EXAMPLE

(1) AWARE. I find comfort in my anxiety in that I am too afraid to do anything in my own behalf. I am conscious that my anxiety about yesterday with its pain, hurt and repressed anger consumes my life today while the anxiety and "what ifs" of tomorrow with its anxiety and fears about what might happen overwhelm me. I am also conscious that by beginning to loosen my "death grip" of living in my own will and letting god move in my life that my anxiety may possibly lessen.

(2) MOTIVATING. I am reading the steps everyday and beginning to see that there is hope for me if I can live in the present and jump out of yesterday and tomorrow. The more I learn how my fears, anxieties are keeping me holed up in my enlarged ego the less possible is it for me to let the Higher Power direct my course. I am developing my faith and learning to let go today.

(3) DOING. I have already admitted I'm depressed and that my life is out of control because of it. Secondly, I came to believe that there is a power greater than myself that is going to restore me to sanity. I have followed step three as suggested and have turned my life and my will over to the care of God as I understand him. I have also learned not to run from my fear but stay and feel it. What I resist persists and gets stronger.

(4) MAINTAINING. My depression and its anxiety lessens the more I speak at DA meetings and share with other members of the group what my fears are. My progress is one day at a time. I am going to make a daily inventory and continually ask God to remove all my shortcomings.

NOW THE WORK BEGINS. YOU PUT THE PUZZLE TOGETHER. FOLLOW THE ABOVE FORMAT AND TRY AND CONSTRUCT AS MANY ANTIDOTES TO ONE'S DEPRESSION THINKING, ACTING AND FEELING AS POSSIBLE.

■4.52 NOW THAT YOU CAN FLY ON YOUR OWN SPEND MUCH TIME WITH EACH OF THE DEFECTS OF CHARACTER THAT YOU WANT USING THE FOUR STAGE PROCESS. YOU MIGHT WANT TO USE A SEPARATE SHEET FOR EACH SHORTCOMING THAT YOU FEEL IS KEEPING YOU DEPRESSED. WHAT EVER YOU DO-- JUST REMEMBER-- TAKE IT ONE STEP AT A TIME. ONE DAY AT A TIME. 1. BE AWARE 2. BE MOTIVATING 3. BE D O I N G 4. BE M A I N T A N I N G

RE-MEMBERING

The healing comes in the telling of the story, the literally painful 'remembering.' As the story is retold and some of the old feelings which were denied and cut off are gradually remembered and received by a supportive and empathic listener, healing starts to happen. The re-membering of the story, particularly if the trauma has been severe and deeply repressed, can be extremely painful, accompanied in some instances by sleep disturbances, nightmares, anxiety or depression. It is critical to let the individual loosen h i s or her own defense of repression at a pace which feels safe, especially as trust is gradually developed....

What are some of the losses of the adult child? He or she has lost childhood in some real w a y s . Very often the growing up in a dysfunctional family means loss of trust and love in some cases and even loss of provision for basic survival needs such as food, shelter and physical safety... Sometimes this chronic depression is masked and defended against by compulsive activity and perfectionist kinds of striving. Becoming " tireless" and "limitless caretakers of others defends a person against his or her own neediness and yearning to be cared for. [14]

REGARDING SELF-CONCEPT AND THE FOURTH STEP

Most of our lives we are involved in relationships of one kind or another. It is these relationships that set us up for being that trusting individual who sees the world either as a safe and secure place to live or we learn to see the world and the people in it as a place to be feared.

Dorothy Rowe, always at her best at helping the depressed develop personal insights asks pertinent questions:

What kind of meaning do you need to find which would enable you to master your experience and so allow you to get on with your life?

What have you learned from your experience of depression which you feel would be helpful to other people?[1]

■4.53 DETERMINE YOUR FEELINGS WHEN YOU REFLECT ON THESE SPECIAL PEOPLE AND H O W T H E I R RELATIONSHIPS AFFECT YOU TODAY, FOR GOOD OR FOR NAUGHT! WRITE THESE FEELINGS OUT!

●●

We have our identity in the process of depressing. We are afraid that if we stop, we won't know how to be, won't know who to be, and won't know what life will expect.

It's safer and more comfortable to continue with the depressing than to risk freedom.

Is this depressing?

Can I realize I do this (reject well-being) without being depressed about it? It's depressing to realize that I've spent my whole life depressing myself.

The most important part is that I've thought it was external. Now I'm getting the sense that it is something I've learned to do and now to do to myself.

To say this is depressing information is like saying that you are on a sinking ship and you have just discovered a lifeboat...

You can stand there and be upset that this ship is sinking or you can take the lifeboat...

We're talking about being compassionate with yourself because everything else springs from that.

It is not selfish to love yourself.

If you can't find compassion for yourself, you'll never find it for anyone else. You won't know how. You will never be truly generous to anyone while depriving yourself.

The reason we don't tell anyone they should do this is that a person won't do this until they are ready.

Most people never will in this life.

All we're saying is that when you're ready here's the way you can do it. This is definitely not another stick to beat yourself.

When you've suffered enough, you'll remember that you know how to do it. It doesn't really matter what you have thought, believed, felt or done before. This is a new day.

"But I've always done it this way." "But I've always been this way." "This is just how I am."

These are three of the world's worst excuses. It's okay to change.

It's okay to try something new.

It's okay to try something radically new... There isn't really anything new because if you try it and don't like it, you can always return to how you were doing it before. No problem. No shoulds. Trying something once or twice doesn't mean you have ever to do it again if you don't want to.

And not taking a risk because you are afraid is a grave disservice to yourself. Fear is not the problem. You can have your fear and allow it to stop you, or you can have your fear and risk anyway. Either way, the fear is there. The choice is yours.[16]

▲▲▲▲▲▲▲▲▲▲▲▲▲▲▲▲▲▲▲▲▲▲▲▲▲▲▲▲▲

PERSONAL CHARACTERISTICS OF SELF-CARE

BY SETTING UP POSITIVE PATTERNS OF THINKING, FEELING AND BEHAVING WE WILL HAVE A MUCH BETTER CHANCE OF LEAVING BEHIND DEPRESSION.

We have made the decision to turn our wills and our lives over to the care of God as we understand Him and this in itself will help us to get honest within ourselves and with the members of the group. This honesty will set us free as we pull ourselves away from the old self that we once were and begin to be in touch with our deepest and truest selves.[17] **(M55)**

■4.54 Write out a description of your old self as compared with the new you that is surfacing because of your involvement with the 12 step program.

And again we read that:

Being socially isolated is a key component in most people's depression. The fact that many depressed people prefer to sit and stew in their isolation and pain precludes their feeling better.[18] **(M58)**

■4.55 Write down all the ways that you found yourself isolating. Can you now detect any patterns in your behavior that lends itself to keeping yourself isolated, be it physically, spiritually or emotionally.

"There is a principle which is a bar against all information, which is proof against all arguments and which cannot fail to keep a man in everlasting ignorance – that principle is contempt prior to investigation."

– Herbert Spencer

In our program of recovery we know that it is only by getting in touch with our feelings --not running from them out of fear --is the start of a new life for ourselves. Steps four, five, six, seven, eight, nine and ten in our program all speak about motivating ourselves to continually work on a daily basis removing the obstacles to personal growth and sanity. If you keep working this program of recovery the promises made to others like yourself will come true and these promises are:

"BOTH YOU AND THE NEW PERSON MUST WALK DAY BY DAY IN THE PATH OF SPIRITUAL PROGRESS. IF YOU PERSIST REMARKABLE THINGS WILL HAPPEN. WHEN WE LOOK BACK, WE REALIZE THAT THE THING WHICH CAME TO US WHEN WE PUT OURSELVES IN GOD'S HANDS WERE BETTER THAN ANYTHING WE COULD HAVE PLANNED. FOLLOW THE DICTATES OF A HIGHER POWER AND YOU WILL PRESENTLY LIVE IN A NEW AND WONDERFUL WORLD, NO MATTER WHAT YOUR PRESENT CIRCUMSTANCES!"[19]

■4.56 Make a list of all the pleasant things you like to do and which are there in your life to do if you so choose --like going for a walk, patting a dog, visiting an art gallery, and so on.

■4.57 Now you are acting as if you are good and valuable, you are doing more things and so discovering more pleasant things to do. Add these to your list as you find them.

■4.58 If you put this list in some place where you can see it before you go to bed, you can check how many pleasant things you have done each day.[20]

■4.59 Please list all the character strengths that you are aware of now but were not aware of till you started your work on this step four.

Step Five

"Admitted to God, to ourselves and to another human being the exact nature of our wrongs."
Step Five of Depressed Anonymous

So many times it is our perfectionism that makes life so difficult and we never seem able to meet the challenge of our own unrealistic goals and ambitions. We never can do it quite well enough.[1] **(M60)**

■5.1 As a child did you get a message that if you were good and did everything that you were supposed to do that you would end up happy and everything would go your way? Write out your response.

■5.2 To be perfect means that everything is under your control. Life is to be predictable and we don't like surprises. We always feel that we are in need of getting everyone's approval for what we do and who we are. Do you feel that yourself worth is based on everyone else' opinion of yourself. Please write out your explanation.

Many times we hear how depression is anger turned inward. This is one way to explain it. Depression is a way to keep from assuming our rightful place in the world and society. You must tell others that your very fear of the future and of others is the very thing that builds your prison.
You need to surrender the fears and hurts of your life...Others in the DA group will also help you see that you can blame the other people in your life for your problems all you want, but it is only when your no longer see yourself as victim that you can stand up and say that you no longer choose to stay depressed. **(M52)**

Step five is about intimacy and the sharing of one's innermost self with its secrets to that other human being. This is something that we hate that we would much rather snuggle back into our little comer and keep all knotted up in the addiction to our misery. In step four we learned about getting it straight within ourselves so that we looked into every nook and cranny inside ourselves that kept us from being honest with ourselves, our god and all the other human beings that we have shared out story with.

■5.3 Can you describe the people that you have c l u n g to in your life--much to your own growth being stunted? Please write about these persons and see if you can find a pattern in the type of persons that you have clung too in the past.

■5.4 Name the persons that you feel you have depended on for more than just social support and fellowship. These would be relationships that are negative and which prevented you from growing,

In step three we made a decision – that is what life is about – namely, making decisions. Our decisions are the product of the meaning that we give to those persons, events and circumstances that fill our lives every day. We make the decisions based on those meanings that we give to those situations and life experiences. We are making a decision today to share part of our dark side w i t h another human being,

In Alcoholics Anonymous it describes the way to make a good fifth step:

We pocket our p r i d e and go to it, illuminating every twist of character, every dark cranny of the past... Once we have taken this step, withholding nothing, we are delighted. We can look the world in the eye. We can be alone at perfect peace and ease. Our fears fall from us. We begin to feel the nearness of our creator. We may have had certain spiritual beliefs, but now we begin to have a spiritual experience...[3]

Telling someone else seems to be the key to our freedom:

When we decided who is to hear our story, we waste no time. We have a written inventory and we are prepared for a long talk. We explain to our partner what we are about to do and why we have to do it.[4]

Step one and step five are the two steps where the word "admitted" is used. When we hear the word "wrongs" such as in this step five – we may induce in ourselves a feeling of guilt. This is NOT the intention of step five at all.

The following are some examples of what we need to write down, viz

■5.5 I want now to list the ways I isolate myself when I feel life is too much for me.

1. EXAMPLE I want to go and lie down and sleep.
2. EXAMPLE I put in more hours at work.
3.
4.
5

THE DEPRESSED ANONYMOUS WORKBOOK

To be depressed is not to be wrong. We are not accusing ourselves as being bad. We only are pointing out the ways that I need to act, think and behave as a non- depressed person.

Moving toward others –

•5.6 Do I set myself up for rejection by being overly dependent on others opinion of me?

•5.7 Do I continually have a chip on my shoulder which prevents others from getting close to me?

•5.8 Does my irritability and hostility serve the purpose of keeping others at arms length from me?

•5.9 Do I move away from people --being afraid to share myself with others.

•5.10 Can I list the ways that I can take more responsibility for myself in my own recovery?

•5.11 I want to list four ways that I plan to take responsibility for myself today. Half of these can be pleasant activities that I will initiate today and the other half will be where I will have some mastery over an activity today that I didn't have yesterday.

■5.11.1

■5.11.2

■5.11.3

■5.11.4

■5.12.1 will make a contract with another personthat I will do one of these activities as proof that I can truly begin to take responsibility for myself.

■5.13 List some of the ways that you have mentally bashed yourself, in the past with such statements such as thinking and saying to yourself that "I'm a fraud, a phony, and worthless."

■5.14 Please list these favorite negative expressions of yourself and then underneath in #b segment list the positive replacements for the negative statement.

■5.14.1a EXAMPLE I can't do anything right!

■5.14.1b EXAMPLE I spoke at a Depressed Anonymous meeting and felt more hopeful!

■5.14.2a

■5.14.2b

■5.14.3a

■5.14.3b

■5.14.4a

■5.14.4b

THE DEPRESSED ANONYMOUS WORKBOOK

■5.14.5a
■5.14.5b

Now please share all of the above with your mentor, sponsor or friend in the program.
■5.15 How are the attempts to be perfect keep us isolated and in the prison of depression?
■5.16 List the ways that you have idealized your self – so that you will never be in touch with your real self-- the spontaneous and free acting self?
■5.17 List the ways that guilt and any past activities in your life made you feel worthless and unacceptable to yourself and to others?

■5.18 In your notebook list five activities that can help make yourself feel acceptable and worthwhile.

■5.18.1
■5.18.2
■5.18.3
■5.18.4
■5.18.5
■5.19 List five things that you are good at? If you can't find five items right away then begin to look more deeply into your life.
■5.19.1
■5.19.2
■5.19.3
■5.19.4
■5.19.5

Depression is also a way to keep from assuming our rightful place in the world of society. You must tell others that your very fear of the future and of others is the very thing that builds your prison.[5] **(M52)**
■5.20 Do you allow yourself to experience anger in your life?
■5.20 With whom are you mad and why are you angry at them. Please list persons and reasons.
■5.20.1
■5.20.2
■5.20.3
■5.20.4
■5.20.5
■5.20.6

THE DEPRESSED ANONYMOUS WORKBOOK

Depressed Anonymous states:

"...Depression feeds on hurt, pain and self-doubt. When we are depressed we have a need to bash ourselves for our misguided errors and sinfulness. The fifth step if done genuinely and prayerfully, will in time help restore our sense of freedom and belief that we are truly forgiven. It is the miracle of the group and its acceptance, love and nurture that helps the depressed person feels secure without recourse to depression."[6] **(M63)**

■5.21 List what action you will have to take if you want to respect yourself again? Remember, it's our past need to tell ourselves how bad and unacceptable that we are that keeps us depressed. This is a "wrong" if there ever was one.

■5.22 Now again, look over and see what your strengths are and what you are doing to take responsibility for helping yourself grow in greater tolerance and love for yourself.

■5.23 Again, list what you have done about your anger, resentments. Can you admit to god that you have been angry with God?
Alienation, self doubt, guilt, shame, hypocrisy, scrutiny – these are the component parts of the cycle of our depression. These five parts that make up the personal construct of being angry at god can be felt by the person depressed at various times. It's a maddening circle of despair.
The fifth step is to take the written fourth step inventory and start with the one that we don't want to share. We take the risk of sharing our deepest defects and shortcomings with another human being and we find that other human being accepts us and forgives.

Our manual states that:

By our continual shutting ourselves up in the little world of our own mind we gradually sink more and more into despair, and feel that no one can understand how we think and feel. The biggest freedom that we can gain from confessing to someone else is that we no longer have to have it all together and be perfect...[7] **(M64)**

■5.24 How has your own need to be perfect helped make your life better? How has being part of a group helped in your gradually coming to be free from depression?

■5.25 What once was blamed on god for one's misery is now seen as our own construction. Can you list those areas of pain in your life which you now claim responsibility for?

Step Six

"We're entirely ready to have God remove all these defects of character."

Step Six of Depressed Anonymous

Once we have dug out in steps four and five what has been the cause of our chronic descent into hopelessness, ewe can not only seek out the solution to our patterns of dysfunction but can now list our strengths.[1] **(M66)**

■6.1 How does pride keep you from facing what needs to be changed in your life today?
■6.2 Write down how you have dropped out of life and so let the sadness take over and rule your life? Spend some time on this.
■6.3 List any persons who were significant to you in the early years of your life who left you by reason of death, divorce or physical separation.

■6.4 Did one of your parents' divorce or abandon you when you were a child. Did you get beat, abused sexually or emotionally. Did others put you down and compare you to brothers or sisters or others and tell you that y o u didn't measure up. If these areas are applicable please write about them now.

NOTE: You might want to go back and look at the responses that you gave to the questions in the Fourth Step Workbook area.

Depressed Anonymous states that:

Many people, for a lot of reasons, are blind to the fact that they are addicted to depression, and continue to live in a state of denial and rationalization about their need to sad themselves. They are saddicts...[2] **(M66)**

■6.5 Discover, describe in your own words how this passage truly speaks to you and how you have indeed saddened yourself? Has being depressed and not making decisions made your life more or less secure?

THE DEPRESSED ANONYMOUS WORKBOOK

Please list below how you might like to respond to these questions. The book further states that:

...So many people choose the predictableness of misery to the risky feeling of being unsure and scared over the new and faint feelings of lightness and cheer. As the depressed person gradually begins to knock down the wall of his or her denial that he or she is addicted to sadness whenever life gets stressful, this in itself is the starting point in the recovery process...[3] **(M66)**

■6.6 What stressful situations or ways of thinking do you want to remove from your life so that you can make a decision to live again!

■6.6.1 to ■6.6.6 (Write out these stressful ways in your notebook).

■6.7 How do I try to please others? How do I plan to change these behaviors? List them.
■6.8 Do I say things, believe things about myself that make me feel small and insignificant? Please list the ways in which I speak to myself words that cause me to continually feel bad about myself.
■6.9 I want to list the various ways that I must talk to myself if I am to keep from sadding myself, and so remain an saddict.
■6.9.1
■6.9.2
■6.9.3
■6.9.4
■6.9.5
■6.9.6 (Please, use your notebook).
■6.10 List the new ways of getting in touch with all my feelings if I am to be free from sadding myself...
■6.10.1
■6.10.2
■6.10.3
■6.10.4
■6.11 List the activities that I am willing to engage in if I am to free myself from the depressive style of life that I am presently living.

■6.11.1

■6.11.2

■6.11.3

■6.11.4

■6.11.5

■6.11.6

■6.12 Dismantling our depression is to take away and tear down a defense that has been a great part of my life for a great part of our lives. it will not be easy to part with some of our behaviors.

Right now list those defects of character that we ask god to rid us of today.

■6.13 Please list what fears are pressing you at this moment. List in order of importance.

■6.13.1

■6.13.2

■6.13.3

■6.13.4

■6.13.5

■6.14 List how you intend to diminish or totally rid yourself of each of the aforementioned fears which still cripple you today?

■6.14.1

■6.14.2

■6.14.3

■6.14.4

■6.14.5

In the AA big book it makes this promise to us who follow this suggested program:

"Both you and the new man (sic) must walk day by day in the path of spiritual progress. If you persist, remarkable things will happen. When you look back, we realize that the things which come to us when we put ourselves in God's hands were better than anything we could have planned. Follow the dictates of a Higher Power and you will presently live in a new and wonderful; world, no matter what your present circumstances."

THE DEPRESSED ANONYMOUS WORKBOOK

The **Big Book of AA** also says:

...we trust an infinite god rather than our finite selves. We are in the world to play the role he assigns. Just to the extent that we do as we think he would love us, and humbly rely on him, does he enable us to match calamity with serenity.[5]

In the manual it states:

...Very deep, sometimes quite forgotten, damaging emotional conflicts persist below the level of consciousness. At the time of these occurrences, they may have given our emotions violenttwists which have since discolored our personalities and altered our lives for the worse.[6] **(M68)**

■6.14 At this point in the Workbook you might want to refer back to the section in Step Four where family of origin issues are discussed in detail. After rereading your comments in that section please list the major areas here and pray to the God of your understanding that these old hurts and memories will now be removed from your life.

■6.15.1
■6.15.2
■6.15.3
■6.15.4
■6.15.5

■6.16 How do I need to take care of myself better physically?

■6.17 Make a list of the ways to help oneself grow healthier physically, spiritually, emotionally.

A. Physically
■6.18.1 Walk (How far per day?)
■6.18.2 Diet (How much of what and when?)
■6.18.3 Relaxation (How and when every day?)

B. Spirituality
■6.19.1 Prayer
■6.19.2 Meditation
■6.19.3 Reading the program literature

C. Emotionally
■6.20.1 Anger and resentment
■6.20.2 Hostility
■6.20.3 Joy and laughter

■6.21 Write how if you wake up tomorrow and you were no longer depressed? What would you feel and what would your life be like?

In the manual it states:

   We have emphasized willingness as being indispensable. Are we now ready to let God remove from us all the things which we have admitted are objectionable? Can he take them all -- every one? If we still cling to something we will not let go, we ask God to help us to be willing ...When ready, we say something like this: "My creator, I am now willing that you should have all of me, good and bad. I pray that you now remove from me every single defect of character which stands in the way of my usefulness to you and my fellows. Grant me strength, as I go out from here, to do your bidding. Amen![7] **(M69)**

■6.22 How do I feel that my recovery from depression can now better suit me for helping those persons still suffering from depression?

Step Seven

"Humbly asked God to remove our shortcomings."
Step Seven of Depressed Anonymous

Now that we have decided to let god remove our shortcomings we see the importance of letting god work in our lives.

We must again let god let go. We really can't do it alone nor can we get over our problems with will power alone.

God wants us to do his will – but it won't be forced onto us – he will work as long as we continue to make a decision to let him into our will and life.

God wants us to do his will – but he won't force us. He will want our hearts and minds.

In our manual it states, quoting Dr. Rowe:

People won't change until they have some assurance that when they do change they will be completely happy. They want to have someone promise them that if they decide to change they will have no more problems and will be happy. Dorothy Rowe says that:

This request is based on two assumptions, namely: 1. Anyone who hasn't got my problems has no problems at all (therefore when my present problems disappear I shall have no problems); 2. Happiness is total certainty (therefore unless I know exactly what is going to happen I cannot be happy).[1] **(M74)**

Change is always difficult. I need to examine in my own life and check out to see if I always expect my actions to produce perfectly happy results or I won't pursue them.

■7.1 Can I write down the activities that I have curtailed over the past years because I thought that I couldn't do them well enough?

If I am honest with myself then I know that life has to be lived as it is and that I will have to make the appropriate choices in my own behalf if my life is to be lived with any kind of joy and spontaneity.

Certainty is so important to us who are or who have been depressed most of our lives. We need the assurance that I can go on living the way I want without fear that the predictability of my life will not be disturbed. The comfort of knowing what I have instead of risking something different is too much of a choice to make for many depressed persons.

Please comment on this passage from Bill W:

"We saw we needn't always be bludgeoned and beaten into humility. It could come quite as much from our voluntary reaching for it as it could from unremitting suffering.....We reach for a little humility, knowing that we shall perish of alcoholism if we do not. After a time, though we may still rebel somewhat, we commence to practice humility because this is the right thing to do. Then comes the day when, finally free in large degree from rebellion, we practice humility because we deeply want it as a way of life."[2]

■7.2 Please write out how humility has been a plus in your own personal recovery from depression?

■7.3 Write a history of your efforts to surrender and let god run your life?

■7.4 List the most important letting go of your life and write out what the result were of letting go and for the depression that imprisoned you?
    As it says in the **AA Big Book,** viz.
    Burn the idea into the consciousness of every man that he can get well regardless of anyone. The only condition is that he trust in God and clean house.[3]

■7.5 In this statement can you find a connection between your own life and how you look at your depression with the hope that it will be gradually eliminated from your life.?

■7.6 From what you have been reading in Depressed Anonymous plus what you hear in the Depressed Anonymous meetings can you now write out and list the different skills which you have gained for yourself since coming to the weekly meetings?
    We have learned from being reading and working the Twelve Steps that there is no easy way out of trying to break out of the cycle of despair that has imprisoned many of us since childhood. It takes humility to admit that we are truly responsible for ourselves and it will take painstaking work to free ourselves from this prison — without bars. Read the next selection and then reflect upon your own experiences.

THE DEPRESSED ANONYMOUS WORKBOOK

   Where humility had formerly stood for a forced feeding on humble pie, it now begins to mean the nourishing ingredient which can give us serenity.

   This improved perception of humility starts another revolutionary change in our outlook. Our eyes begin to open to the immense values which have come straight out of painful ego puncturing. Until now, our lives have been largely devoted to running from pain and problems.

   We fled from them as from a plague. We never wanted to deal with the fact of suffering....Then in A.A., we looked and listened. Everywhere we saw failure and misery transformed by humility into priceless assets. We heard story after story of how humility had brought strength out of weakness. In every case, pain had been the price of admission into a new life. But this admission price had purchased more than we expected. It brought a measure of humility, which we soon discovered to be a healer of pain. We began to fear pain less, and desire humility more than ever.[4]

■7.7 What keeps me from relapsing back into depression?

■7.7.1 PERSONAL COMMENTS ON WHAT THIS STATEMENT MEANS TO YOU.

■7.8 Please write about how you heard about Depressed Anonymous, what your first meeting was like and what you have been feeling since that first meeting. Also what were your impressions about the Depressed Anonymous manual after your first reading?

   The building blocks of staying out of the way of danger with depression is to be open, honest, and willing to do something different than what we have been doing.

■7.9 How open have I been to talk with trust to those in the meetings?

■7.10 List those persons and their phone numbers who you consider to be your social support to keep you from being re hospitalized or prevent you.

■7.10.2

■7.10.3

■7.10.4

■7.10.5

■7.11 Notice that we have asked God to remove our shortcomings. Notice the step doesn't say remove our sins – but instead we are asking god to remove our shortcomings. Do you personally consider sin as interchangeable with the term shortcoming? Please explain your answer

Depressed Anonymous states:
...finally we believe that humility is the rock on which each of the twelve steps of Depressed Anonymous is based.[5] **(M77)**

■7.12 Can you list your reasons why this statement is to be true?

We know that the English word, "humility" comes from the Latin word "humus", which means the earth. If we are honest and humble we then will be true to ourselves and to others. We will no longer continue to deny the facts about our addiction to sadness, and tell ourselves that the only thing that we need to do is just take some pills and we'll be alright....But pills canno remove the reason for the pain nor can they remove our shortcomings. We have to face the truth and admit that somehow I am the cause of my depression...[6] **(M71)**

■7.13 Please write out a response to the above statement.

Have you been aware of any changes inside of you the more you begin to look at your life from the perspective of the twelve steps? Is it possible that you u n c o v e r more of your real self the more you attend meetings and share with others the material in this Workbook?

■7.14 Please record your response to the following:

We reacted more strongly to frustrations than normal people. By reliving these episodes and discussing them in strict confidence with somebody else, we can reduce their size and therefore their potency in the unconscious.[7]

■7.15.1

■7.15.2

■7.15.3

■7.15.4

...We have to face the truth and admit that somehow I am the cause of my depression...[8] **(M71)**

Now that you have thoroughly worked through steps four and five you surely have been able to come up the various ways that you have chosen to depress yourself.

■7.16 Do you think that you are worthless and a fraud? Why or why not?

■7.17 Do you still try and please everyone around you?

■7.18 Do you feel hostile toward others? Please explain your reasons for the responses to these questions.

■7.19 To be humble means to be truthful – do you feel that you are dealing with yourself truthfully?

THE DEPRESSED ANONYMOUS WORKBOOK

The **AA Big Book** says:

"...Are we now ready to let god remove from us all the things which we have admitted are objectionable? Can He now take them all -- every one? If we still cling to something we will not let go, we ask God to help us be willing. When ready, we say something like this: "My creator, I am now willing that you should have all of me, good and bad. I pray that you remove from me every single defect of character which stands in the way of my usefulness to you and my fellows."[9]

■7.20 By this prayer we now invite you to list some of the character defects that you feel you have been working on since you began this 12 step program of Depressed Anonymous?

■7.20.1

■7.20.2

■7.20.3

Dr. Rowe comments that:

"In an order to establish whether or not you are an extrovert or an introvert, really a very important distinction and an important understanding of oneself, it is good to establish just who we are and how we see the world. "Are you an extrovert or an introvert? If you have not already worked this out, choose something that you do which is important. It might be skiing, or cleaning your car, or being in a choir, or reading newspapers, visiting friends --anything."

■7.21 Now ask yourself, 'Why is this important?', and write down the reason.

■7.22 Now look at the reason and ask yourself, ' Why is this important?'

Go on asking this question and examining the reasons until you come to the answer which shows what you see as the purpose of your life and what you see as the greatest threat to you.

If, in answering these questions, you say, 'It makes me feel good', or 'It's pleasant', or, 'It's stimulating' or 'I enjoy it', work out just what you mean by 'feeling good', or 'pleasant', or 'stimulating', or 'enjoyable'. For instance, by 'feeling good' do you mean a feeling in relationship to other people, or a feeling of achieving something? With achieving, some people (extroverts) achieve as part of their relationships – being accepted into the group, not being rejected, being the center of attention, being admired and loved by many people -- while at the same time trying not to be so successful as to attract enmity and rejection from the members of their group. Other people (introverts) achieve for themselves. They are pleased when the people they approve of approve of them, but the person they want most to approve of their achievement is themselves. Being rejected by others because they are so successful might hurt them, but it is not a major concern which would prevent them from achieving. High a c h i e v i n g , o r w o u l d b e achieving, introverts believe that anyone who does not agree with them and does not approve of what they do is a fool. Remember that what you are examining is not what you do but *why you do it...*[10] (306-307).

Dr. Rowe continues with her questions:

■7.23 Write a list of all the people in your life who are important to you (remembering that people who give us a really bad time are as important to us as those who give us a good time because they interfere in our life).

■7.24 Beside each name put which you think they each are, an introvert or an extrovert.

Then, when you have the opportunity, get them to tell you what they see as the purpose of t h e i r life and what they fear most. You might be able to ask some of them this directly, although with others you will have to slide in that revealing question, "Why is that important?'

■7.25 How many did you get right?

■7.26 What words do you use to refer to your sense of badness and unacceptability?
Turn your thought inwards and focus on how you experience yourself as bad and unacceptable using your own words. Let the image you have of this come clearly to mind.[11]
Images play a big part in our life – even those images that have residual pieces lodged in our memories. These images still can fire up our feelings and we don't know from whence they came. These are dated images that come packaged in feelings – mostly feelings of sadness and anxiety. These feelings sometimes are happy i m a g e s . Smells u s u a l l y p r e d a t e images and images produced b y smells usually go way back.

■7.27 Can you think of images that caused you anguish, and hurt as a child. List these and see if you can quietly recreate these images and see what feelings come with them.
■7.27.1
■7.27.2
■7.27.3

■7.27.3

■7.28 List them in the order of importance to you today.

Again, we want to ask god to remove any fears or specters from the past that today still live and influence us today.

In our manual it says that:

Depressed Anonymous is a place to clean house, forgive ourselves and others, and begin to depend on God as we understand Him. We need to develop a God consciousness...[12] **(M47)**

■7.29 Now that we have thought over and prayed about our need to have God help us remove our shortcomings what positive steps have you taken in this Workbook step to further God's continued and daily work in your life so that you don't relapse back in to your old thinking and behavioral ways for depressing yourself? Please list these positive steps below!

■7.29.1

■7.29.2

■7.29.3

■7.29.4

■7.29.5

Step Eight

"Made a list of all persons we had harmed, and became willing to make amends to them all."
Step Eight of Depressed Anonymous.

In **Depressed Anonymous** it states:
One of the dead – end s t r e e t s that addicted people travel down – often at breakneck speeds – is to blame everyone else for their problems.[1] **(M78)**

In your own quiet time, can you think of anyone that you might blame for your problems today such as any institution, the government, the Church, an employer a family member such as a parent, spouse, brother, sister or stepparent?

Most of us have harmed someone in our life and because we are depressed doesn't mean that this is absent from our lives. It seems that harm is a big issue in our lives especially as it has to do with our relationships past and present. This step gives us the opportunity to go back and look at all our lives and take the opportunity to acknowledge where we were wrong and promptly admitted it. It is indeed a cleansing process. This is an occasion where we can get at the root of our problems and at the same time discover the p a t t e r n of how our r e l a t i o n s h i p s have ended in a predictable f a s h i o n. It also may demonstrate how our relationships have all been with someone that was like the rest of our failed relationships.

This step eight also gets us in touch with how our failed relationships coupled with our own character defects have thrown us back into depression.

■8.1 Can you describe how one's own feelings about past failed relationships have made you feel shame, guilt or anxiety. List the ways they made you feel and write them down. Our manual it states t h a t:

And if we are going to treat depression like any other addiction such as alcoholism, gambling, sexual and love addictions, or overeating then why not call ourselves what we are, namely, saddicts. If the alcoholic can recover so can the saddict?[2] **(M80)**

■8.2 How do you feel about being a saddict ? List the ways that keep you saddicted?

■8.2.1

■8.2.2

THE DEPRESSED ANONYMOUS WORKBOOK

■8.2.3

■8.2.4

■8.2.5

■8.2.6

■8.2.7

■8.2.8

■8.2.9

■8.30   List the activities /ways that can free you from your depression addiction.

■8.30.1

■8.30.2

■8.30.3

■8.30.4

■8.30.5

■8.30.6

■8.30.7

■8.30.8

Can you relate to the following statement?

"Our only enemies are guilt, fear and shame. Such unresolved n e g a t i v e s prevent us from living fully."[3]

Elizabeth Kubler-Ross

■8.3 Write down in 8.3 as much as you care, about how depression has prevented you from really living? Then in part 8.31B write down how the 12 step program has increased your ability to live free and with joy?

■8.31A

■8.31B

We do not become enlightened by imagining figures of light, but by making the darkness conscious. –Carl Jung

■8.32 Write down any habits that seem to drive you and put you in the passenger seat instead of in the driver's seat?

■8.33 Please write about your guilt w h i c h is centered on acts that h a d b e e n committed against others and for w h i c h I could not and would not forgive myself. Please list these people and describe what it would mean to be free from the guilt that you feel about these actions.

THE DEPRESSED ANONYMOUS WORKBOOK

When we understand that we may want to blame someone or some agency or institution for what has happened to us --such as an unloving parent we need to realize that this grudge, resentment has to be gotten rid of if we are to move out of an into the freedom of love and life.

■8.34 Can you name the person(s) that you usually blame for your problems today?

■8.35 Write down all the things that this person inflicted upon you and the way it made you feel?

In the 3rd grade a teacher told me how I would never be like an older brother. I always have carried the message around with me down through the years and how bad that made me feel --how unacceptable it made me feel about myself, Now, I no longer feel that way, because I am me. I believe now that God has given me talents that have helped me be who I am and who I am to become.

■8.36 Write down how your own depression has kept you disconnected from others?

We then need to make amends to those whom we have harmed – sometimes this can be unintentional because our drives are unconscious and driven by the dated emotions such as early childhood fears of being abandoned, rejected, feeling worthless. Also we might add that if you have been sad and depressed over any length of time just know that it has adversely affected people around you.[4] (M79)

Again we don't want to blame ourselves here but we do need to take responsibility for the way we feel, think and act as this all belongs to us and so we must claim it.

■8.37 What person or persons has my "sadness fear and social isolation affected...?"[5] (M79)

■8.38 List the ways that my sadness has kept me from risking new adventures in my life?

■8.39 List the ways that my fears have kept me from career positions or advances in my life's work and dreams.

■8.40 List the ways) that my social isolation has kept me disconnected from my family, friends and relationships in general?

As a means of discovering yourself Dorothy Rowe would have us:

■8.41 Write down the experiences you have had which made you feel that you were, in your own words, bad and unacceptable. This exercise is one that you will need to come back to as you remember different things. (Your answers to this exercise could be the essence of a best-selling novel, or an autobiography which your nearest and dearest will pay you a large sum of money not to publish.)

■8.42 Choose one of these experiences from childhood and tell the story twice, once from the point of view of you as a child and once from the point of view of you as an adult... "Which of these ways of preserving yourself did you choose?

■8.43 "As you were growing up you were constructing what the story of your life would be. Write this story down...[6] **(301-302)**

Dr. Rowe continues with more questions:

■8.44 Now that you've written down your plans, write the story of your life.

■8.45 Now look at the places where those two stories diverge and make a list of these.

■8.46 Which of these divergence's make you feel pleased?

■8.47 Which of these divergence's make you feel disappointed?

■8.48 Which of these divergence's make you feel angry and resentful?

■8.49 Which of these divergence's make you feel frightened? [7](307-308)

■8.50 Please write out just where is it that you feel you might tend to live the most in the past. How old were you then? What was going on at that time of your life?

What do you think about the statement?

We know by painful experience that the depressed person puts a lot of stock in the past and has a tendency to live there.[8] **(M81)**

Further on it says:

... I believed no one could love me for just me. We really never fully trusted anyone, and that included our God, our religious leaders, our spouses, our children, our best friends.[9] **(M83)**

■8.51 Has this changed now that you have made the mutual – aid group Depressed Anonymous such a big part of your life? Describe in your own words how you may be trusting others more with the varied areas of your life, both pleasant and unpleasant!

Step Nine

"Made direct amends to such people where ever possible, except when to do so would injure them or others."

Step Nine of Depressed Anonymous

The Big Book of Alcoholics Anonymous states:

We have a list of all persons we have harmed and to whom we are willing to make amends. We made it when we took inventory. We subjected ourselves to a drastic self-appraisal. Now we go out to our fellows and repair the damage done in the past. We attempt to sweep away the debris which has accumulated out of our effort to live on self-will and run the show ourselves. If we haven't the will to do this, we ask until it comes. Remember it was agreed at the beginning we would go to any lengths for victory over alcohol.[1] (76)

Again, Alcoholics Anonymous states:

Our real purpose is to fit ourselves to be of maximum service to God and the people about us. It's seldom wise to approach an individual who still smarts from our injustice to him, and announce that we have gone religious...[2]

It also says later on that:

....we will never get over drinking (depression, gambling, etc.) until we have done our utmost to straighten out the past.
Now that we have admitted our past mistakes and said we were willing to make amends to them all we now actually do this and put into action the spirit of this step.[3]
■9.1 Please comment in your own words on this sentence in our manual:
So often our depression hides behind a mask of superficial friendliness – with people never aware of the deep pain that we feel inside. The risk is in moving out of isolation into contact with other depressed people. We know now that it is the expression of our feelings that gets us free. It is the telling and the admission of our powerlessness over our depression that makes us move ever so slowly out of

the deep pit of darkness and sadness. So often when we are able to make amends we feel that part of the prison wall begins to crumble and we begin to see the light of day. We discover a way out! We find that our forgiveness of others frees us and brings us one more step into the peace of serenity.[4] **(M85-86)**

■9.2 How much are you willing to tell someone how your depressed behavior has kept you from choosing to be more responsible for your health, and your life as a whole?

■9.3 Please write how has my negative and passive behavior caused harm to others?

■9.4 Need I make amends to myself for fearing to express my anger when it needed to be expressed? Do I still think it is wrong to get angry?

■9.5 How can I believe that the best path out of depression is to get active in talking to others about depression and letting them know how relieved we are to be able to talk about our depression. List the people that you plan to share with this week about your depression?

The manual states that:

...(The list must be prayed over and reflected upon so that we can do the proper Spring cleaning and have the peace and the serenity promised to those to take responsibility for their own actions.[5] **(M84)**

■9.6 Please comment on this statement and ask yourself how much responsibility that you have over your depression?

The manual continues to say that:

...(We also might be tempted to fight for our personal pride at times, falsely thinking that we really don't need to make amends to anyone and that we are just fine the way we are.[6] **(M85)**

If we think that we are fine just the way we are then we do have a problem.

Dorothy Rowe in her book, **Depression: The way out of your prison** tells us that:

Dangers, perhaps even greater dangers, threaten you if you leave your prison of depression for the ordinary world. There you might have to change, and change always involves uncertainty. The good thing about being depressed is that you can make every day the same. You can be sure of what is going to happen. You can ward off all those people and events that expect a response from you. Your prison life has a regular routine, and like any long term prisoner, you grow accustomed to the jail's security and predictability. The prison of depression may not be comfortable, but at least it is safe.[7]

■9.7 Please write down how this paragraph speaks to you or doesn't speak to you. Spend some time on it as it is a crucial truth!

Dorothy Rowe states that:

Given the choice, you would prefer to be right and suffer than wrong and happy. As you well know, when we say we are wrong we create an area of uncertainty. If what I thought proves to be wrong, then a whole range of possibilities immediately opens up and it might be some considerable time before I can discover which of these possibilities is right. If you cannot tolerate uncertainty then you cannot afford to admit that you are wrong.

Absolute certainty may appear to you to be a wonderful thing, giving complete security, but have you ever considered that if you want absolute certainty you must give up freedom, love and hope?[8]

Dr. Rowe continues:

...pride, so Christian theology teaches, is the deadliest of the seven sins since it prevents the person from recognizing his sins and repenting and reforming. Sin or not, it is pride that keeps you locked in the prison of depression. It is pride that prevents you from changing and finding your way out of the prison.[9]

■9.8 Which of the following can you best relate?

You take pride in seeing yourself as essentially bad; you take pride in not having and accepting other people; pride in the starkness and harshness of your philosophy of life;
1. Pride in the sorrows of your past and the bleakness of your future;
2. Pride in recognizing the evil of anger;
3. Pride in not forgiving;
4. Pride in your humility;
5. Pride in your high standards;
6. Pride in your sensitivity;
7. Pride in your refusal to lose face by being rejected;
8. Pride in your pessimism;
9. Pride in your martyrdom;
10. Pride in your suffering.[10]

■9.9 Instead of seeing depression as something caused by external circumstances and oneself playing no actual part in its makeup do you take Rowe's statement as a blaming stance? Do you feel that you had nothing to do with your depression or the fact that it continues to keep you isolated and disconnected from life? Do you really believe you had no part in its formation in your life? Please comment!

THE DEPRESSED ANONYMOUS WORKBOOK

The Depressed Anonymous manual states that:

"...Once I admit that I am addicted to depressing myself then I can begin to walk through the door of the prison that binds me. I must realize the fact that my depression will only get worse unless I put a stop to all the thinking, feeling and acting out behavior that keeps me perpetually locked into my sadness?"[11] **(M87)**

Here again we see the responsibility issue cropping up again. This is so important for us who want to hide and run when we feel a life that has to be risked again and again. As we read in the book Alcoholics Anonymous and as quoted in Depressed Anonymous:

"Our real purpose is to fit ourselves to be of maximum service to god and the people about us....

Yes, there is a long period of reconstruction ahead. We must take the lead. A remorseful mumbling that we are sorry won't fill the bill at all...[12] **(M88)**.

It continues:

One of the better ways to make amends is to commit yourself on a daily basis to helping other members of the DA group find peace and serenity.

If there is anything that we learn in Depressed Anonymous it is the friends that we make in the fellowship and the help that we are able to give others even when we ourselves feel we are sinking below the surface...[13] **(M88).**

■9.10 Can we list the new friends that we have made since we started our meetings of Depressed Anonymous. List and write about the one person in the group that you admire the most. Please give reasons why the group and this person mean so much to you?

Step Ten

"Continued to take personal inventory and when we were wrong promptly admitted it."

Step Ten of Depressed Anonymous

What do I do when I feel that I have done somebody or done something wrong? We can take an inventory during the day and or at the end if day to see how our lives have gone. **Our manual says that:**

"As we continue to keep ourselves free of the thoughts that imprison us ever more tightly with our depression, we begin to recognize that this power greater than ourselves can and will restore us to sanity."[1] **(M89)**

■10.1 Please list how since participating in Depressed Anonymous that your life has become more balanced and more sane?
The manual says:

...We need to do the grief work and mourn this loss in our early life. And so grieving a loss goes through a number of predictable stages and these stages must be experienced if one is to experience a life free of the sadness that might have been hurting for many years.[2] **(M90)**

Is there someone who was close to you as a child who died but whom you did not grieve or shed a tear for because you were still too young to say that you missed their love and their presence. All of a sudden they were gone and you suddenly got on with your life but your body remembered that this person was once a meaningful part of your life. This might take some investigative work on you part but talk to family and friends and see if there were deaths around the time that you were growing up and which you were unaware of but might have affected your parents or guardian's perception of life and so affected you.

■10.2 Please jot down any ideas that you might have about these thoughts.

■10.3 Have you ever felt abandoned as a child that you can remember? Did you feel loved and secure as a child growing up?

The **Twelve Steps and Twelve Traditions** states:
...We need not be discouraged when we fall in to the error of our old ways, for these disciplines are not easy. We shall look for progress, not for perfection.

■10.4 Write down the ways that you think that you might try and be perfect? Also write down the effect this need to be perfect has had on your life and your relationships?

The **Twelve Steps and Twelve Traditions** likewise says:
...One unkind tirade or one willful snap judgment can ruin our relation with another person for a whole day, or maybe a whole year. Nothing pays off like restraint of tongue...[4]

■10.5 How have you felt your tongue has been restrained enough or not enough?

The **Twelve Steps and Twelve Traditions** also states:
...We must avoid quick-tempered criticism and furious power-driven argument. The same goes for sulking or silent scorn. These are emotional booby traps baited with pride and vengefulness...[5]

■10.6 Please comment on the above and write about how these apply to you
   In the manual it states that:
   Responsibility is the name of the game in recovery and it is here that we need to focus our attention. As we get into a discussion with other people who are depressed-- much like ourselves – we see that they talk about feeling better while at the same time acting on their own behalf. These people who are doing better are also talking about taking charge of their lives and doing things for themselves instead of constantly trying to please others.[6]**(M91)**

■10.7 Write out in your own words how life was before you came to Depressed Anonymous?

■10.8 Have you seen a change in yourself since being a part of Depressed Anonymous? Has the taking charge of yourself and your feelings been a help in getting free from depression?

■10.9In what areas of your life have you had to take charge and change? List your major fears that you might have if you made major changes in your life? What if any might you have guilt feelings about? What if any might you feal anxious about right now?

Dorothy Rowe states that:
As you well know, when we say we are wrong we create an area of uncertainty... if you cannot tolerate uncertainty then you cannot afford to admit that you are wrong. Absolute certainty may appear to you to be a wonderful thing, giving complete security, but have you ever considered that if you want absolute certainty you must give up freedom. love and hope.[7]

■10.10 What do you think has kept you locked up in your prison of depression? What have you not dared to change that has kept you a prisoner of your depression? How can we take the necessary steps to change the ways that we might interpret things?

■10.10 As we continue this inventory can we think of any incident in our adult life that continually 'makes us sad (Christmas holidays?) that we might connect with a childhood circumstance.
NOTE: ☺☺☹   This personal inventory is taken on a daily basis not as a way to shame us but a way to help us arrive more smoothly at a point of keeping our lives balanced and free from sadness.

■10.12 Please comment on the following statement from the AA Big Book:
...We vigorously commenced this way of living as we cleaned up the past. We have entered the world of the Spirit. Our next function is to grow in understanding and effectiveness. This is not an overnight matter. It should continue for a lifetime. Continue to watch for selfishness, dishonesty, resentment, and fear. When these crop up, we ask God at once to remove them. We discuss them with someone immediately and make amends quickly if we have harmed anyone. Then we resolutely turn our thoughts to someone we can help. Love and tolerance of others is our code....Every day is a day when we must carry the vision of God's will into all our activities. "How can I best serve Thee? Thy will (not mine) be done" These are the thoughts which must go with us constantly. We can exercise our will power along this line all we wish. It is the proper use of the will.[8]

■10.13 List the new and positive ways that you have been thinking of yourself lately?

■10.13.1

■10.13.2

■10.13.3

■10.13.4

■10.13.5

■10.14 List the people from your Depressed Anonymous group that you would like to talk to today.

■10.14.1

■10.14.2

■10.14.3

■10.14.4

■10.14.5

■10.15 List the various pleasant activities that you are planning to engage in these next few days:

■10.16 Write down the activity that you will undertake plus the particular day that you plan to accomplish this activity.

■10.16.1

■10.16.2

■10.16.3

■10.16.4

■10.16.5

■10.17 On a scale of one to ten rate which of the following emotions ruled the day for you. (1 denotes lowest dominance while 10 ranks as highest dominating force.)

Anger Worry Guilt Fear

■10.18 Now list the various ways that you plan to remove your most frequent unpleasant emotion? Write down your strategy!

The **Depressed Anonymous** manual states that:

Promptly forgive ourselves! Promptly tell a friend, DA group member, coworker, spouse, that you are now trying to live one day, one hour at a time and are depending on the Higher Power to give you the courage to risk thinking hopeful thoughts which have the power to lead yourself back into the community, the family and among friends. Develop a gratitude attitude and thank God for today! This day is all we have. Get involved in your own healing. Start to take on

THE DEPRESSED ANONYMOUS WORKBOOK

the attitude that if other people can make it then so can I. It's true – you can make it if you follow the program.[9] **(M94)**

■10.19 List ten things that you are grateful for today and each day following, please list one more thing that you are grateful for.
■10.19.1
■10.19.2
■10.19.3
■10.19.4
■10.19.5
■10.19.6
■10.19.7
■10.19.8
■10.19.9
■10.19.10

THE DEPRESSED ANONYMOUS WORKBOOK

Step Eleven

"SOUGHT THROUGH PRAYER AND MEDITATION TO IMPROVE OUR CONSCIOUS CONTACT WITH GOD AS WE UNDERSTOOD GOD, PRAYING ONLY FOR KNOWLEDGE OF GOD'S WILL FOR US AND THE POWER TO CARRY THAT OUT."

Step Eleven of Depressed Anonymous

In Depressed Anonymous the statement is made:
With our compulsion to sad ourselves, much like the alcoholic's urge to medicate him or herself with alcohol, we need daily to turn our will over to God and ask for the Higher Power's guidance. Eventually it is the conscious contact with this loving God that sets us free from the need to sad ourselves.[1] **(M95)**

■11.1 Question: How do you see your depression as a compulsion? What are the triggers that cause you to spiral downward back into the dark pit of depression?

When you think of depression do you think of it like one big thing or do you see it for the many parts that make up a depression experience, namely, the way that we think, behave, or feel. In other words when we make it to be a thing that is when we reify it – it holds power over us – like it came out of the blue – we talk about depression in medical terms such as I just had a bout of depression – like it came from outside of us like an infectious germ or virus. In reality, our depression is made up of many parts, such as particular depressiogenic ways of thinking, behaving and feeling.

■11.1 Write the way that you perceive your depression? Can you distinguish the various parts that go to form what we call the depression experience?

■Which of the following illustrations can you best relate to"

■11.1A need to be perfect!

■11.2A need to be successful!

■11.3 A need to please others – always!

■11.4 A need never to get angry!

■11.5 A need to have someone in my life before I feel I am somebody!

■11.6 Please write down how one or more of the above keeps you down, despairing and hopeless? Also, write about where these attitudes came from?

THE IDEALIZED IMAGE

The idealized image is a decided hindrance to growth because it either denies shortcomings or merely condemns them. Genuine ideals make for humility, the idealized image for arrogance.[2]

All of our efforts so far in this workbook have been directed toward overcoming our shortcomings – cleaning house if you will – so that our will might be properly disposed to God's will and that we might feel free and no longer hopeless. We know that our enthusiasm to change will grow the more we desire that change. The more we change the more we will cast off the shackles from our lives that keep us imprisoned and bound.

Please respond to the statement:
I can't do anything to remove my compulsive behavior until I choose to 'live without it. It is truly living in the will and mind of god that will help us, one day at a time to stop being so compulsive in our rigid and automated thinking about people and things so that we do not let our dated emotions and thoughts predict what the outcome of our perceptions ought to be.[3] **(M95)**

■11.7 Please list in the order of their importance what you are doing now that you were not doing before you came into Depressed Anonymous.
■11.7.1
■11.7.2
■11.7.3
■11.7.4
■11.7.5
■11.8 Tell how this new way of living with the 12 steps of Depressed Anonymous is making life worth living again!

■11.9 Do you find yourself less fearful and no longer automatically sadding yourself when faced with new situations and new challenges? Yes or no. If yes please explain.

■11.10How do you feel about the statement:

If we haven't ever been big on "organized religion" we have a good chance that this new approach to being with god is much less judgmental, and that this God of the twelve steps is much more accepting than other concepts of god that we might once have held.[4] **(M99)**

Beginning with step three, we discovered that when we finally surrendered our wills and out lives over to the care of god of our understanding that this was a step in trust – and action. It's as if once we reframed this god of ours into a loving and caring god it was much easier then to turn our lives over to this new image of a god once so mighty, distant and uncaring.

■11.11 Write out the various words that best describe this god of your understanding. Please likewise relate how the group that you are part of has helped you find acceptance, love and mercy from this god of your understanding.

A comment from AA Grapevine:

...The faith of my Sunday School days was gone, and "the god of my understanding" was far off. (But not so far as I thought, as it turned out.) It stretched me to even imagine" a power strength and I became willing to take this route. I wasn't ready to take on God just yet.

However, god was ready to take me on, for in my ignorance I'd done about all that AA asks – I had become willing. And this is how he did it. In some casual reading about seeds, this statement caught my attention:" Science can construct a seed identical to a natural seed in every detail but one – science's seed will not germinate." The words seemed to leap from the page. They demanded answers. What is the missing ingredient in the manmade seed? Is it some dimension I don't know about? Is it in everything? Even people? And then the big question. Who is in charge here, anyway?

Backed in to a corner finally, by a logic greater than my ego, I conceded. Too many miracles, too much coincidence, and too much evidence of a power greater than myself all around me left me defenseless and in awe. I surrendered. And the power wasted no time in reinforcing my new belief with these words from the Big Book: "We found that as soon as we were able to lay aside prejudice and express even a willingness to believe in a power greater than ourselves, we commenced to get results, even though it was impossible for any of us to fully define or comprehend that Power, which is God.....

..He is always there if I but look, feel and want him to be; my conscious contact is dependent upon my being willing.[5]

■11.12 How willing are you now to continue the progress that you have made so far? Please write down how willing you are to help your fellow sufferers of depression in Depressed Anonymous.

■11.13 Write how you can be of greater service to the newcomer and those who are isolating and withdrawing from the groups support.

A new life of endless possibilities can be lived if we are willing to continue our awakening.[6]

■11.14 How do you plan to continue your personal awakening?

The cornerstone of Depressed Anonymous is one depressed person helping another, to paraphrase AA's saying.

Our manual states that:

Steps Two and Three, like Step Eleven, are concerned with our wills being in God's will. We should seek, as a priority, a knowledge of His will for us. But the recovery is up to you...[7] **(M99)**

■11.15 List the ways that you attempt to be in God's will. As far as you are concerned relate how you can begin to tell that you are in god's will?

Our manual says:

...We want only to know God's will because if your will is lined up with God's will, then everything that you need or want is all there. It's very liberating to desire only that your will be in God's' will. The more you pray, the more you will want to be in God's will. Your saddiction will be a thing of the past and the peace of God will be a thing of the now.[8] **(M102)**

■11.16 Please write how your life has shown any marked changes since you have lined up your will with God's?

The manual says that:

Getting free from our saddiction is to learn how to prize ourselves.[9] **(M102)**

■11.17 List the ways that you have learned how to prize yourself after having participated in Depressed Anonymous and having begun to work the steps.

THE DEPRESSED ANONYMOUS WORKBOOK

- ■11.17.1
- ■11.17.2
- ■11.17.3
- ■11.17.4
- ■11.17.5

Bill W. says that:

"In praying, our immediate temptation will be to ask for specific solutions to specific problems, and for the ability to help other people as we have already thought they should be helped. In that case, we are asking god to do it our way. Therefore, we ought to consider each request carefully to see what its real merit is.

Even so, when making specific requests, it will be well to add to each of them this qualification: if it be thy will.[10]

Another good way to maintain our "conscious contact" with God is to read the daily meditation book titled **HIGHER THOUGHTS FOR DOWN DAYS**[11], as this will keep you focused on the positive avenues that one must travel' if one is to escape depression. Whatever happens we all need to find that quiet place where we can rest and listen. Listen means to be silent. I personally believe that the more silence we keep the more God will allow his love, his peace seep into every nook and cranny of our hurting psyche and cleanse us of fear and hurt...

This step is all about being empowered! It is much like the saying in the Russian Proverb that "We must pray but also keep rowing to shore!"

In the manual, quoting the Big Book of AA it states:

There is a principle which is a bar against all information, which is proof against all arguments and which cannot fail to keep a man in everlasting ignorance – that principle is contempt prior to investigation.[12] **(M99)**

Have you truly tried the various avenues of healing that have been laid out for you in Depressed Anonymous meetings?

■11.18 if the answer is yes, please write down all the ways that this has helped you.
   Our manual states that:

We conclude that since our depression and sad thoughts are getting progressively worse over the course of time, we then have to admit that our feelings are out of control and that we need help.[13] **(M99)**

■11.19 When we listen we learn and to learn means to keep listening. Is there anything today that you have learned by listening? Write down what you have heard that specially applies to you today. Write down what you have learned.

Dorothy Rowe wrote:

Dangers, perhaps even greater dangers, threaten you if you leave your prison of depression for the ordinary world. There you might have to change, and change always involves uncertainty. The good thing about being depressed is that you can make every day be the same. You can be sure of what is going to happen. You can ward off all those people and events that expect a response from you. Your prison life has a regular routine, and like any long-term prisoner, you grow accustomed to the jails security and predictability. The prison of depression may not be comfortable, but at least it is safe.[14]

■11.20 Please respond to the comments above and give your own reactions. Has your conscious contact with God given you a greater sense of freedom and such that in time you will escape the prison of depression?

■11.21 Write down your thoughts and listen as the God of your understanding speak to you. Step Eleven is a hopeful step in that it prays that god will give us the power to carry out all that is necessary to carry out so that we can get where god wants us to be. This will only happen when we take the time every day, the same place and making it a regular routine where we can slowly remove the bars that keep us locked up' in the prison of our depression. We now have the keys to release ourselves.

■11.22 Now write down how you are going to get started today as you begin to prayer and meditate so that you may make conscious contact with GOD...

Step Twelve

"Having had a spiritual awakening as the result o f these steps, we tried to carry this message to others and to practice these Principles in all of our affairs."

Step Twelve of Depressed Anonymous

■12.1 Write down what comes to mind when you hear the word Awakening? Have you experienced an awakening now that you have spent some time working the 12 steps and going to the Depressed Anonymous meetings.

■12.2 Write down how this awakening has been spiritual? How do you define spiritual for your own life?

■12.3 Who have you told about Depressed Anonymous in the last week? Write down who it was with whom you talked to about your depression and how the 12 step' program that has changed your life?
  Our manual states:
  Depressed Anonymous want you and me to try for one day at a time not to withdraw compulsively into sadness when we come up against a stressful situation.[1] **(M105)**

■12.4 Has there been a stressful situation such a s a death, a loss of a loved one or loss of a job that you have experienced that is causing you to be depressed? How has your involvement with Depressed Anonymous kept you from compulsively relapsing back into your depression? Write the ways this social support group has helped you from climbing back into the deep dark pit of depression.
  This spiritual awakening is what has enabled us to admit our failings, look at our character defects and get on with learning how to live out our life. This spiritual awakening also allows us to expect something good to happen for once instead of something bad --as in the past. It also allows us our feelings back.
The part about carrying the message is so important if we are to remain out of the clutches of depression. It is important to keep in touch with the newcomers and others in the program. It is this carrying the message that reminds us that we once needed help and it was through the unselfishness of the older members of Depressed Anonymous that got us through our depression

THE DEPRESSED ANONYMOUS WORKBOOK

■12.5 Please write out how you are practicing the principles of Depressed Anonymous in all of your affairs. Write out a one paragraph statement what your life was before Depressed Anonymous and what it is like now that you are involved in the program?

■12.6 Write down the time of day that you spend with God as you understand God.

■12.7 Write down the five people on your phone list that you would like to keep in contact with this week.

■12.7.1
■12.7.2
■12.7.3
■12.7.4
■12.7.5

■12.8 Please comment on this quote from the AA Big Book:

"Both you and the new man (woman) must walk day by day in the path of spiritual progress. If you persist, remarkable things will happen. When we look back, we realize that things which came to us when we put ourselves in god's hands were better than anything we could have planned. Follow the dictates of a Higher Power and you will presently live in a new and wonderful world, no matter what your present circumstances."[2]

And in another place the Big Book of AA says:

If I were asked what in my opinion was the most important factor in being successful in this program besides following the Twelve Steps, I would say Honesty. And the most important person to be honest with is Yourself...[3] (367-368)

■12.9 How has your honesty with yourself made your life more free and more fulfilled with hope? Write down the areas of your life where you feel your honesty has paid the richest dividends? How has honesty made your life less needful of pleasing others so that they will like you or accept you more?

■12.10 "How does our own "Honesty" help us "carry the message" to others still hurting? Please write out your response.

THE DEPRESSED ANONYMOUS WORKBOOK

Our **Depressed Anonymous** manual states that:

We all know that any addiction and compulsive type of behavior removes you from the regular activities of persons around you, including family, friends and coworkers, until you are established in the narrow confines of pain and isolation...[4] **(M105)**

■12.11 Have you noticed that you are spending less and less time alone and more time with others as friendships and the fellowship grows among you and others that you have met in Depressed Anonymous? Please write your thoughts on this matter.

Our addictive nature says that we are never going to feel better and that it is safe only to stay where we are and not risk anything different that we already know.

■12.12 What do you think and feel when you read the following passage?

...And anytime we want to stop and reflect on how badly other people have treated us, we need to reflect on what we are doing to ourselves by all this negative rehashing...[5] **(M108)**

I believe that since we have begun working this program that we now are able to stop ourselves in this mad rehashing and take responsibility for the fact that we don't have to think this way. We can now replace the negative with something positive.

■12.13 List all the negative things that you at an earlier time used to beat yourself up with? As we know, this is a compulsion that indirectly puts us back where we feel comfortable – namely, back into the pit of our depression. Our minds and bodies are so used to getting back in the neural rut of badmouthing ourselves that it will take time and practice to stop the negative and put positive thoughts into our minds.

■12.14 List the positive affirmations that you will have ready when you begin to bash yourself.
■12.14.1
■12.14.2
■12.14.3
■12.14.4
■12.14.5 (Five affirmations)

■12.15 Name some of the people that you have shared your story of hope with this week.
■12.15.1
■12.15.2
■12.15.3

The following is a good summary of all the steps and it might do us well to make a comment on how our lives relates to the individual step as outlined in

THE TWELVE STEPS AND TWELVE TRADITIONS.

Step one showed us an amazing paradox: We found that we were totally unable to be rid of the depression obsession until we first admitted that we were powerless over it.[6]

■12.16 Question: Have you felt any hopelessness recently and if so what might be the reason as far as you know?
In Step Two we saw that since we could not restore ourselves to sanity, some Higher Power must necessarily do so if we were to survive.[7]

■12.17 Question: In what ways do you feel that you have been restored to sanity? In other words what was insane about your thinking, feeling and behavior? Consequently, in Step Three we turned our will and our lives over to the care of God as we understood Him. For the time being, we who were atheist or agnostic discovered that our own group, or A.A. as a whole, would suffice as a higher power.

■12.18 Question: How does the Higher Power bring you daily out of your depression? Is the Higher Power your best friend? How is that so and how did that come about?
Beginning with Step Four, we commenced to search out the things in ourselves which had brought us physical, moral, and spiritual bankruptcy. We made a searching and fearless moral inventory.[8]

■12.19 Question: Is there any area in our lives today that we would say is suffering from bankruptcy as like the time that we first came into the program? Do I continually keep at the search to ferret out those persons, place and thoughts that try and keep me isolated and depressed?

Looking at Step Five, we decided that an inventory, taken alone, wouldn't be enough. We knew we had to quit the deadly business of living alone with our conflicts, and in honesty confide these to god and another human being.

■12.20 Question: How have I solved my personal conflicts today? Do I find that when I share my story and my troubles in the group that somehow my life feels lighter for the trip to a meeting?

At Step Six, many of us balked – for the practical reason that we did not wish to have all our defects of character removed, because we still loved some of them too much. Yet we knew we had to make a settlement with the fundamental principle of Step Six. So we decided that while we still had some flaws of character that we could not yet relinquish, we ought nevertheless to quit our stubborn, rebellious hanging on to them. We said to ourselves, "This I cannot do today, perhaps, but I can stop crying out "No, never!"[9]

■12.21 Question: Are there any defects of character that you still find most difficult to eradicate from yourself. Name what they are and share this with the group or write down the ways that you will take care of these matters so that you can finally give up the familiar and the predictable and begin to live with some risk.

Then, in Step Seven, we humbly asked God to remove our shortcomings such as He could or would under the conditions of the day we asked.[10]

■12.22 Question: What shortcoming would you consider to be the most important to be removed as soon as possible?

In Step Eight, we continued our housecleaning, for we saw that we were not only in conflict with ourselves, but also with people and situations in the world in which we lived. We had to begin to make our peace, and so we listed the people we had harmed and became willing to set things right.[11]

■12.23 Question: How has your spiritual awakening been enhanced by "carrying the message" to others still suffering from depression? Is there anyone that you need to make peace with today?

We followed this up in Step Nine by making direct amends to those concerned, except when it would injure them or other people...[12]

■12.24 Question: How has making direct amends helped you in your ongoing spiritual awakening?

By this time at Step Ten, we had begun to get a basis for daily living, and we keenly realized that we would need to continue taking personal inventory, and when in the wrong we ought to promptly admit it.[13]

■12.25 Question: What is your basis for daily living? Write down if you are rising earlier, taking care of yourself better and getting more exercise than ever before? Now that you are actively working the program?

In Step Eleven we saw that if a Higher Power had restored us to sanity and had enabled us to live with some peace of mind in a sorely troubled world, then such a Higher Power was worth knowing better, by as direct contact as; possible. The persistent use of meditation and prayer, we found did open the channel so that where there had been a trickle, there now was a river which led to sure power and safe guidance from God as we were increasingly better able to understand him.[14]

■12.26 Question: If someone asked you how you knew there was some for real Higher Power what would you tell them about your own personal experiences that might help them believe that truly there is a Power greater than ourselves.

Hope is what we seek as people depressed. We refuse to label ourselves as depressives because we do not intend to be depressed any longer than we have to. We are also a lot more than our feelings of sadness. Our real identity is emerging from the sadness as we try to live one day at a time.[15] **(M164)**

■12.27 Question: It appears that when we push down our emotions that all our emotions are affected and that nothing happy or cheerful is ever to be brought into our life, but if we try and become more hopeful then our outlook on life begins to take a change for the better and we see that there is hope and that joy may be possible once again. It's like we are wearing glasses that have only gray to be seen – no colors.

■12.28 Who are you? Please describe as best you can your real self? Also write down the characteristics of the self you want to be but aren't? How different are the two?

■12.29 Please answer if there is a way you can make some changes here.

THE DEPRESSED ANONYMOUS WORKBOOK

Depressed Anonymous is not the place to have people feel sorry for you. Depressed Anonymous is a spiritual program where you will find people like yourself, honestly, openly and willingly dealing with their character defects and gradually admitting that they will have to change their lives and lifestyle if they are going to be a whole and honest human being. The decision is yours. You make the choice! The twelve steps and your own personal story can now be shared with others and can help them on their own life'sjoumey.[16] **(M108)**

Please close this phase of the Workbook assignment by commenting on this passage:

"If we are painstaking about this phase of our development, we will be amazed before we are halfway through. We are going to know a new happiness. We will not regret the past nor wish to shut the door on it. We will comprehend the word "serenity" and we will know peace. No matter how far down the scale we have gone, we will see how our experience can benefit others. That feeling of uselessness and self-pity will disappear. We will lose interest in selfish things and gain interest in our fellows. Self seeking will slip away. Our whole attitude and outlook upon life will change. Fear of people and economic insecurity will leave us. We will intuitively know how to handle situations which used to baffle us. We will suddenly realize that God is doing for us what we could not do for ourselves....

Are these extravagant promises? We think not. They are being fulfilled among us-- sometimes quickly, sometimes slowly. They will always materialize if we work for them."[17] **(M109)**

■12.30 Please share your thoughts about how much your life has changed because of the painstaking work that you have invested in your own life and world. Write out the positive results as if you were sharing your testimony at a Depressed Anonymous meeting and especially directing your remarks at the newcomer – the one who as yet doesn't know the choices that he/she will make will either continue to imprison them or free them from the chains of depression. How has the spiritual program of Depressed Anonymous set you free?

THE END

Bibliography

STEP ONE

1.   Depressed Anonymous, Harmony House Publishers, Prospect, KY, 1998, page 35.

2.   Ibid., 35.

3.   Ibid., 31.

STEP TWO

1.   Dorothy Rowe, *Depression: The Way Out of Your Prison,* Routledge, 1983, 56.

2.   Depressed Anonymous, 43.

3.   Ibid., 55.

4.   Ibid., 45-46.

5.   Hugh Smith, 15 Statements of Belief, Louisville, 1995, 16.

STEP THREE

1.   Depressed Anonymous, 52.

2.   Ibid., 52.

3.   Ibid., 53.

4.   Ibid., 54.

5.   Ibid., 56.

6.   Dorothy Rowe, Breaking the Bonds, HarperCollins, London, 1991, 311.

THE DEPRESSED ANONYMOUS WORKBOOK

7.   A Co-Founder of AA, *As Bill Sees It: The A.A. Way of Life: Selected Writings of A.A.'s Co-Founder,* Alcoholics Anonymous World Services, Inc., New York, 1967, 331.

8.   Ibid., 331.

9.   Ibid., 72.

10. A Co-Founder of AA, Twelve Steps and Twelve Traditions, Alcoholics Anonymous World Services, Inc., New York, 1953, p.38.

11. Ibid., 35.

12. Ibid., 41-42.

13. Depressed Anonymous, 58.

14. A Co-Founder of AA, As Bill Sees It, 117.

15. Ibid., 304.

16. Ibid., 304

17. Ibid., 253.

18. Depressed Anonymous, 57.

19. *A Co-Founder of AA, As Bill Sees It,* 321.

STEP FOUR

1.   The Depression Book: Depression As An Opportunity For Spiritual Practice, 1991, pages 113 – 114.

2.   Depressed Anonymous, 61.

3.   Ibid., 59.

4.   Twelve Steps and Twelve Traditions, 44.

5.   Ibid., 98.

6.   Alcoholics Anonymous: The Story of How Men and Women Have Recovered from *Alcoholism,* Alcoholics Anonymous World Services, Inc., New York, 1955, 64-65.

THE DEPRESSED ANONYMOUS WORKBOOK

7. Rowe, Depression: The Way Out of Your Prison, 15-16.

8. *Alcoholics Anonymous,* 67, 69.

9. Women's Treatment Handbook, Domestic Abuse Program, Duluth, Minnesota, 1991.

10. Depressed Anonymous, 61

11. Albert Ellis, *Reason and Emotion in Psychotherapy,* Lyle Stuart, New York, 1962.

12. Jill Anderson, Thinking, Changing, Rearranging: Improve Self-Esteem in Young People, Timberline Press, Eugene, OR, 51, 52.

13. Rea Me Donnell & Richard Callahan, CSC., Adult Children of Alcoholics: Ministers and Ministries, Integration Books, Paulist Press, New York, 1990, 33,45,114.

14. Rowe, *Breaking the Bonds,* 318.

15. *The Depression Book: Depression As An Opportunity for Spiritual Practice,* 1991, 113 – 114.

16. Depressed Anonymous, 63.

17. Ibid., 64.

18. *Alcoholics Anonymous,* 100.

19. Rowe, *Breaking the Bonds,* 320.

STEP FIVE

1. Depressed Anonymous, 68.

2. Ibid, 70.

3. *Alcoholics Anonymous,* 103.

4. Ibid., 102.

5. Depressed Anonymous, 70.

6. Ibid., 70.

7. Ibid., 72.

THE DEPRESSED ANONYMOUS WORKBOOK

8.   Ibid., 73.

STEP SIX

1.   Depressed Anonymous, 76.

2.   Ibid., 76.

3.   Ibid., 76.

4.   *Alcoholics Anonymous,* 100.

5.   Ibid.68.

6.   Depressed Anonymous. 78.

7.   Ibid., 81.

STEP SEVEN

1.   Depressed Anonymous, 86.

2.   *As Bill Sees It,* 211.

3.   *Alcoholics Anonymous,* 98.

4.   *Twelve Steps and Twelve Traditions,* 76.

5.   Depressed Anonymous, 90.

6.   Ibid., 83.

7.   *Twelve Steps and Twelve Traditions,* 111.

8.   Depressed Anonymous, 83.

9.   *Alcoholics Anonymous,* 76.

10. Rowe, *Breaking the Bonds,* 306-307.

11. Ibid., 307.

12. Depressed Anonymous, 53.

STEP EIGHT

1. Depressed Anonymous, 91.

2. Ibid., 93

3. Elizabeth Kubler-Ross, *On Death and Dying,* New York: Macmillan, 1969, 121.

4. Depressed Anonymous, 91.

5. Rowe, *Breaking The Bonds,* 301-302.

6. Ibid., 307-308.

7. Depressed Anonymous, 95.

8. Ibid., 97.

STEP NINE

1. *Alcoholics Anonymous,* 76.

2. Ibid., 77.

3. Ibid., 77.

4. Depressed Anonymous, 99.

5. Ibid., 99.

6. Ibid., 97.

7. Dorothy, Rowe. Depression: The Way out of your prison, 127.

8. Ibid., 128-129.

9. Ibid., 129.

THE DEPRESSED ANONYMOUS WORKBOOK

10. Rowe, *Depression: The Way Out of Your Prison,* 129.

11. Depressed Anonymous, 101.

12. Ibid., 103.

13. Ibid., 102.

STEP TEN

1. Depressed Anonymous, 104.

2. Ibid., 105.

3. *Twelve Steps and Twelve Traditions,* 93.

4. Ibid., 93.

5. Ibid., 94.

6. Depressed Anonymous, 107.

7. Rowe, *Depression: The Way Out of Your Prison,* 152

8. *Alcoholics Anonymous,* 84-85.

9. Depressed Anonymous, 110.

STEP ELEVEN

1. Depressed Anonymous, 111.

2. Karen Horney, M.D., *Our Inner Conflicts: A Construction Theory of Neurosis,* 1945, W.W. Norton & Company, NY, 98-99.

3. Depressed Anonymous, 111.

4. Ibid., 112.

5. *The Grapevine,* December, 1995, 8-9.

6. *The Grapevine,* 1957.

7.   Depressed Anonymous, 116.

8.   Ibid., 119.

9.   Ibid., 120.

10. *As Bill Sees It,* 329.

11. Hugh Smith, *Higher Thoughts For Down Days,* Louisville, 1993.

12. Depressed Anonymous, 116.

13. Ibid., 116.

14. Rowe, *Depression: The Way Out of Your Prison,* 127.

STEP TWELVE

1.   Depressed Anonymous, 121-122.

2.   *Alcoholics Anonymous,* 100.

3.   Ibid., 367-368.

4.   Depressed Anonymous, 123.

5.   Ibid., 126.

6.   *Twelve Steps and Twelve Traditions,* 110-112.

7.   Ibid.,

8.   Depressed Anonymous, 125.

9.   Twelve steps and Twelve Traditions, 70.

10. Ibid., 75.

11. Ibid., 79.

12. Ibid., 86.

13. Ibid., 92.

14. Ibid., 101.

15. Depressed Anonymous, 122.

16. Ibid., 126.

17. Ibid., 127.

THE DEPRESSED ANONYMOUS WORKBOOK

For more information about Depressed Anonymous
Please contact us at the following web address:

Http://www.depressedanon.com

Or write:

**Depressed Anonymous Publications
PO Box 17414
Louisville, Kentucky 40217**

Order Form

Description	Price	Qty	Total
Depressed Anonymous Twelve Step Guide and testimonials.	$15.00		
The Depressed Anonymous Workbook Working the 12 Steps one at a time.	$12.00		
Higher Thoughts for Down Days 365 Daily Uplifting Thoughts and Meditations for those in recovery.	$18.00		
TeenCare How to prize oneself.	$10.00		
Seniorwise Group program for those older and growing. Includes Leader's Manual.	$18.00		
How to Find Hope! A short lesson in living.	$4.00		
Depressed Once-Not Twice! Special Introduction to Depressed Anonymous for Newcomers.	$7.00		
Shining A Light on the Dark Night of the Soul A short treatise on how to remove the guilt and shame voice.	$5.00		
The Promise of Depressed Anonymous For those who live the 12 Steps of recovery.	$5.00		
Dep-Anon Family Group Manual A 12 Step Program for those whose family members or friends are depressed.	$10.00		
Believing Is Seeing? 15 Ways to leave the prison of depression.	$7.00		
I'll Do It When I Feel Better This 150 page work contains Ten Chapters. There is an introduction by the author as well as a first chapter giving an overview of the book.	$14.00		
		Sub Total	
		Shipping& Handling $4.95 per order	
		TOTAL	

Make Check/Money Order/Western Union Payable to: Depressed Anonymous
Send to: PO Box 17414
Louisville, KY 40217

Include:
Name_____
Address_____
City, State, Zip_____
Phone_____

Made in the USA
Charleston, SC
31 May 2015